Mastering C++ the Easy Way

Step-by-Step Projects and Concepts for Absolute Beginners

Booker Blunt

Rafael Sanders

Miguel Farmer

Boozman Richard

How to Scan a Barcode to Get a Repository

1. **Install a QR/Barcode Scanner** – Ensure you have a barcode or QR code scanner app installed on your smartphone or use a built-in scanner in **GitHub, GitLab, or Bitbucket.**

2. **Open the Scanner** – Launch the scanner app and grant necessary camera permissions.

3. **Scan the Barcode** – Align the barcode within the scanning frame. The scanner will automatically detect and process it.

4. **Follow the Link** – The scanned result will display a **URL to the repository**. Tap the link to open it in your web browser or Git client.

5. **Clone the Repository** – Use **Git clone** with the provided URL to download the repository to your local machine.

Chapter 1: Introduction to C++ Programming

Objective:

This chapter serves as a fundamental introduction to the world of C++ programming. It aims to demystify the core concepts of programming and provide a gentle yet thorough introduction to the C++ language for absolute beginners. Whether you're a complete novice to programming or looking to expand your skill set, this chapter will guide you through the basics, helping you set up the development environment, understand the structure of a C++ program, and ultimately run your first program. By the end of this chapter, you will be familiar with the tools you need and the syntax used in C++, enabling you to start writing and executing simple programs.

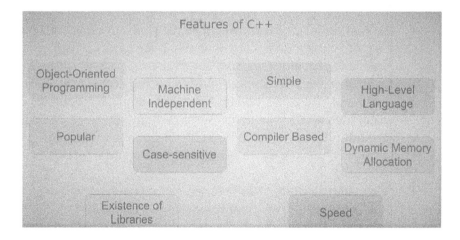

What is C++?

C++ is a high-level programming language that is widely known for its power and versatility. It was developed by Bjarne Stroustrup in the early 1980s as an enhancement to the C programming language, introducing object-oriented programming (OOP) features. The language allows you to perform a wide range of tasks, from building operating systems and games to developing applications for desktop, mobile, and embedded systems.

One of the key aspects that set C++ apart from other languages is its support for both high-level and low-level programming. It provides features that let you work directly with hardware, such as pointers and manual memory management, which gives you more control over the system's resources. This makes C++ an excellent choice for tasks that require performance optimization, like real-time systems or graphics programming.

Why C++?

- **Performance**: C++ is known for its high performance, making it a go-to choice for applications that need to run at high speeds or with strict memory constraints.
- **Control**: It gives developers fine-grained control over system resources, which is crucial in fields like game development, embedded systems, and hardware programming.
- **Versatility**: From developing web applications to desktop software and large-scale systems, C++ is adaptable for many use cases.
- **Wide Adoption**: C++ has been in use for over four decades, and its ecosystem includes a wide variety of libraries, frameworks, and tools. This makes it a valuable language to learn for future career opportunities.

The C++ Development Environment: Setting Up IDEs and Compilers

Before diving into writing and running your first program, it's essential to set up a proper development environment. This involves installing an Integrated Development Environment (IDE) and a C++ compiler. The IDE is a tool where you will write, compile, and run your C++ programs, while the compiler translates your code into machine-readable instructions.

Installing an IDE

Here are two popular IDEs for C++ development that you can use:

1. **Visual Studio**:
   Visual Studio is one of the most widely used IDEs for C++ development. It offers powerful features like IntelliSense (code completion), a debugger, and integrated tools for version control and testing. Visual Studio works best on Windows, though a version for macOS is also available.
   - **Step 1**: Download Visual Studio from the official website.
   - **Step 2**: During installation, select the "Desktop development with C++" workload to install the necessary tools for C++.
   - **Step 3**: Once installed, you can start a new C++ project from the Visual Studio dashboard.
2. **Code::Blocks**:
   Code::Blocks is a free, open-source IDE that works on Windows, Linux, and macOS. It is lightweight and easy to use, making it ideal for beginners. It supports multiple compilers, including GCC (GNU Compiler Collection), which is commonly used for C++ development.
   - **Step 1**: Download Code::Blocks from the official website.

- o **Step 2**: Install the IDE along with the included GCC compiler.
- o **Step 3**: Once installed, you can create a new project by selecting "Console Application" and choosing C++.

Installing a C++ Compiler

If you don't choose an IDE that comes with a compiler, you'll need to install one manually. Here are a couple of options:

- **GCC**: The GNU Compiler Collection is one of the most popular open-source compilers for C++.
  - o On Windows, you can use **MinGW** (Minimalist GNU for Windows) to install GCC.
  - o On Linux or macOS, GCC is typically pre-installed or can be installed using package managers like `apt` or `brew`.
- **Clang**: Clang is another C++ compiler that works on multiple platforms and is known for its fast compilation speed. It is widely used on macOS, and it's possible to install it on Windows and Linux as well.

Once the compiler is installed, you can compile C++ programs from the command line by typing `g++ your_program.cpp -o output` (for GCC) or `clang++ your_program.cpp -o output` (for Clang).

First Steps: Writing and Running Your First C++ Program

Now that you have the tools set up, it's time to write your very first C++ program. This will be a simple program that prints "Hello, World!" to the screen. It may seem basic, but it's an essential first step in understanding how to work with C++.

Code Explanation:

cpp

```
#include <iostream>   // This line includes the
input/output stream library.

int main() {   // The main function, where the program
starts.

    std::cout << "Hello, World!" << std::endl;   //
Output text to the screen.

    return 0;   // Exit the program with a return
value of 0, indicating success.
}
```

Breaking Down the Code:

- `#include <iostream>`: This line tells the compiler to include the "iostream" library, which allows us to use input and output features like printing text to the screen.
- `int main()`: This defines the main function, which is the entry point of any C++ program. When you run a C++ program, the execution always starts from the `main()` function.
- `std::cout`: This is the standard output stream in C++, used to print data to the screen. The `<<` operator is used to send data to `std::cout`.
- `"Hello, World!"`: This is a string literal. It's the text that will be displayed on the screen.
- `std::endl`: This inserts a newline after the text, making the output more readable.
- `return 0;`: The return statement ends the program and sends a status code back to the operating system. A return value of 0 indicates that the program ran successfully.

<u>Running the Program:</u>

- **In Visual Studio**: After writing the code, click the "Run" button (green arrow) to compile and execute the program. The output should appear in the terminal window.
- **In Code::Blocks**: Similarly, click the "Build and Run" button to compile and execute the program.

Once you run the program, you should see the text "Hello, World!" printed in the terminal.

Basic Syntax and Structure: Understanding C++ Syntax and the Structure of a C++ Program

Now that you've successfully written your first program, it's time to understand the underlying syntax and structure that makes a C++ program work. Here, we'll break down the important elements of C++ syntax to give you a strong foundation for writing more complex programs.

<u>Syntax Basics:</u>

- **Statements**: C++ programs are made up of statements, which are individual commands or instructions. A statement is usually terminated with a semicolon (;).
- **Comments**: Comments are notes that are added to the code for clarification and are ignored by the compiler. They are written using / / for single-line comments or / * . . . * / for multi-line comments.
  - Example:

    ```cpp
    // This is a single-line comment
    /* This is a
    ```

```
multi-line comment */
```

The Structure of a C++ Program:

Every C++ program has a basic structure. At its simplest, a C++ program consists of:

1. **Preprocessor Directives**: These are instructions that are processed before the program starts running. The `#include` directive, for example, tells the compiler to include external libraries or header files.
2. **Main Function**: Every C++ program has a `main()` function. This is where execution begins.
3. **Statements and Expressions**: Inside the main function, you'll write the code that defines what the program does. This can include variable declarations, function calls, and mathematical expressions.
4. **Return Statement**: Most programs end with a `return 0;` statement that indicates the program has executed successfully.

Project: Your First Program – "Hello World"

Let's revisit the goal of this chapter by working on a simple yet meaningful project: the "Hello World" program. As you already know, this project prints "Hello, World!" to the screen. In this project, we'll build on that knowledge by introducing more features, including basic data input and output, to make the program a little more interactive.

Project Objective:
In this extended version of the "Hello World" program, the user will input their name, and the program will print a personalized greeting.

Code:
cpp

```cpp
#include <iostream>
#include <string>  // This library is required for
working with strings

int main() {
    std::string name;   // Declare a variable to store
the user's name

    // Prompt the user to enter their name
    std::cout << "Please enter your name: ";

    // Get the user's input and store it in the
'name' variable
    std::getline(std::cin, name);

    // Output a personalized greeting
    std::cout << "Hello, " << name << "! Welcome to
C++ programming." << std::endl;

    return 0;   // End of program
}
```

Code Explanation:

- `#include <string>`: This includes the `string` library, which allows us to work with string data types.
- `std::getline(std::cin, name);`: This function reads a full line of input, including spaces, and stores it in the `name` variable.

Steps:

1. Compile and run the program.
2. When prompted, type your name and press Enter.
3. The program will greet you by name.

Conclusion of Chapter 1

By now, you have successfully:

- Installed the necessary tools for C++ development.
- Written your first C++ program and executed it.
- Gained an understanding of the basic syntax and structure of C++.
- Worked on a hands-on project to reinforce these concepts.

In the next chapter, we will explore **Variables, Data Types, and Constants**, which are crucial for storing and manipulating data in your programs. But before moving on, remember that programming is a journey. Every step you take brings you closer to mastering C++, and the more you practice, the better you'll become. Keep experimenting and coding!

Chapter 2: Variables, Data Types, and Constants

Objective:
In this chapter, we will focus on foundational concepts that are essential for any C++ programmer: **variables, data types**, and **constants**. By the end of this chapter, you will be able to declare and use variables of different types, understand how data is stored in memory, and use constants to handle unchanging values. To bring these concepts to life, we'll build a simple calculator program that allows users to input numbers and perform basic mathematical operations like addition, subtraction, multiplication, and division.

What are Variables?

Variables are a fundamental concept in programming. Think of them as containers or storage locations in memory where we can store values that can change as the program runs. In C++, every variable must be declared with a specific type before it can be used. This type defines what kind of data the variable will store.

Declaring a Variable

To declare a variable in C++, you specify the **data type** followed by the **variable name**. Here's the basic syntax:

```cpp
data_type variable_name;
```

For example:

```cpp
int age;
double price;
char grade;
```

In this code:

- `int age;` declares a variable named `age` that will store an integer value.
- `double price;` declares a variable named `price` to store a floating-point number.
- `char grade;` declares a variable named `grade` to store a single character.

Variables are stored in memory, and the data type you choose for a variable dictates how much memory it will consume and what kind of values it can hold. For example, an `int` takes up 4 bytes in memory (on most systems) and stores whole numbers, while a `double` takes 8 bytes and can store decimal numbers.

Assigning a Value to a Variable

Once a variable is declared, you can assign a value to it. This is done using the assignment operator `=`:

```cpp
int age = 25;
double price = 19.99;
char grade = 'A';
```

In this code:

- `age` is assigned the value `25`.
- `price` is assigned the value `19.99`.
- `grade` is assigned the character `'A'`.

Variable Names

When choosing variable names, there are a few important rules and best practices:

1. Variable names should be meaningful, so they reflect the data they store.
2. A variable name cannot begin with a number. For example, `1stNumber` is invalid, but `firstNumber` is valid.
3. You cannot use C++ keywords as variable names (e.g., `int`, `double`, `return`).
4. It's common practice to use camelCase for multi-word variables (e.g., `userAge`, `totalPrice`).

Common Data Types in C++

Data types in C++ define the kind of data a variable can hold. Each data type has a specific size in memory and a defined range of values. Let's take a closer look at some of the most common data types in C++:

1. int

The `int` data type is used to store whole numbers (integers). It can hold positive and negative numbers, as well as zero.

- **Size**: 4 bytes (on most systems).
- **Range**: Typically -2,147,483,648 to 2,147,483,647.

Example:

```cpp
int age = 30;
```

2. double

The `double` data type is used to store decimal numbers (floating-point numbers). It can represent both very small and very large numbers.

- **Size**: 8 bytes.
- **Range**: Approximately ±1.7E±308, with 15–16 decimal digits of precision.

Example:

cpp

```cpp
double pi = 3.14159;
```

3. char

The `char` data type is used to store a single character, such as a letter, digit, or symbol. It is usually enclosed in single quotes.

- **Size**: 1 byte.
- **Range**: Typically -128 to 127 (signed) or 0 to 255 (unsigned).

Example:

cpp

```cpp
char grade = 'A';
```

4. bool

The `bool` data type is used to store **boolean values**, representing **true** or **false**.

- **Size**: 1 byte (although the exact size can vary by implementation).
- **Range**: Only two values: `true` or `false`.

Example:

```
cpp

bool isStudent = true;
```

Constants and Literals

Constants are values that do not change during the execution of a program. They are useful when you have values that are used multiple times in your code, and you want to ensure they don't accidentally get modified.

Defining Constants

In C++, you can define constants in two ways:

1. **Using the `const` keyword**:
    The `const` keyword is used to declare a constant variable. Once assigned, the value cannot be changed.

    ```
    cpp

    const double pi = 3.14159;
    ```

    In this example, `pi` is a constant variable of type `double` with a value of `3.14159`. Once set, you cannot change the value of `pi`.

2. **Using `#define` preprocessor directive**:
    The `#define` directive is another way to define constants, commonly used for values that are replaced at compile-time.

    ```
    cpp

    #define MAX_SIZE 100
    ```

Here, `MAX_SIZE` is defined as a constant with the value `100`. Whenever `MAX_SIZE` is used in the code, it is replaced with `100` during the compilation process.

Literals

A literal is a fixed value used directly in your code. You've already seen several examples of literals in the previous section. For example:

- `25` is an integer literal.
- `3.14` is a floating-point literal.
- `'A'` is a character literal.

C++ has different types of literals based on the data type:

- **Integer literals:** `int num = 10;`
- **Floating-point literals:** `double pi = 3.14159;`
- **Character literals:** `char letter = 'A';`
- **Boolean literals:** `bool flag = true;`

Project: Building a Simple Calculator

Now that we have covered variables, data types, and constants, it's time to put everything into practice by creating a simple calculator that can perform basic math operations. This will allow us to interact with variables, take user input, and use conditional statements to perform different operations.

Project Objective:

Create a console-based calculator that:

- Takes two numbers as input from the user.

- Offers a choice of four basic operations: addition, subtraction, multiplication, and division.
- Displays the result of the selected operation.

Code Implementation:

cpp

```cpp
#include <iostream>
using namespace std;

int main() {
    double num1, num2;   // Declare two variables to
store the numbers
    char operation;       // Declare a variable to
store the operation symbol

    // Ask the user for two numbers
    cout << "Enter first number: ";
    cin >> num1;
    cout << "Enter second number: ";
    cin >> num2;

    // Ask the user to choose an operation
    cout << "Choose an operation (+, -, *, /): ";
    cin >> operation;

    // Perform the operation based on user input
    if (operation == '+') {
        cout << "Result: " << num1 + num2 << endl;
    }
    else if (operation == '-') {
        cout << "Result: " << num1 - num2 << endl;
    }
    else if (operation == '*') {
        cout << "Result: " << num1 * num2 << endl;
    }
    else if (operation == '/') {
        if (num2 != 0) {
            cout << "Result: " << num1 / num2 <<
endl;
        } else {
            cout << "Error: Division by zero is not
allowed!" << endl;
```

```
        }
    }
    else {
        cout << "Invalid operation!" << endl;
    }

    return 0;
}
```

Explanation of the Code:

- **Variables**: We declare two `double` variables, `num1` and `num2`, to store the numbers input by the user. The `char` variable `operation` stores the selected operation symbol.
- **User Input**: The `cin` statement is used to read user input for the numbers and the operation.
- **Conditional Statements**: Based on the user's operation choice, an `if-else` block is used to perform the appropriate calculation:
    - If the user selects addition (+), the program adds `num1` and `num2`.
    - If the user selects subtraction (-), the program subtracts `num2` from `num1`.
    - If multiplication (*) is selected, the program multiplies the two numbers.
    - If division (/) is selected, the program checks if `num2` is not zero before performing the division. If `num2` is zero, an error message is displayed.

Test the Calculator:

To test your calculator:

1. Run the program.
2. Enter two numbers and choose an operation.
3. The program will display the result of the chosen operation.

Conclusion

In this chapter, you have learned the key concepts of variables, data types, and constants in C++. You have explored how to declare variables, assign values to them, and use them to store different types of data. You also built a practical calculator project that allowed you to apply these concepts in a real-world scenario.

In the next chapter, we will dive deeper into **Control Flow** and **Decision Making** in C++, learning how to write programs that can make decisions and repeat tasks. Stay tuned for more engaging examples and hands-on projects as we continue our journey through C++ programming.

Chapter 3: Control Flow - Decision Making

Objective:
In this chapter, we will introduce you to **control flow** in C++ programming, specifically focusing on decision-making structures. Decision-making structures allow your program to execute certain blocks of code based on specific conditions. By the end of this chapter, you will understand how to use **if statements, if-else** chains, and **switch-case** statements. You will also be introduced to **logical operators**, learn how to create **nested if statements**, and work on a **project** to build a number guessing game, which will allow you to apply these concepts.

What is Control Flow?

Control flow is one of the most essential concepts in programming. It refers to the order in which individual statements, instructions, or function calls are executed or evaluated. In C++, control flow allows you to specify different paths that a program can take based on certain conditions. Without control flow, a program would simply execute line by line without making decisions.

The primary way to control flow in C++ is through **decision-making** constructs, which evaluate conditions (expressions that return true or false) and then decide whether to execute a block of code.

If Statements

The **if statement** is the most fundamental way to make decisions in C++. It executes a block of code only if a specified condition is **true**. The condition is an expression that evaluates to either `true` or `false`.

Basic Syntax:

cpp

```
if (condition) {
    // Code to execute if the condition is true
}
```

For example:

cpp

```
int age = 20;
if (age >= 18) {
    cout << "You are an adult." << endl;
}
```

In this code:

- The condition `age >= 18` is checked.
- If the condition is true (in this case, `age` is 20), the program prints `"You are an adult."`.

How It Works:

- If the condition evaluates to **true**, the code inside the curly braces `{ }` will execute.
- If the condition evaluates to **false**, the code inside the braces will be skipped, and the program continues with the next line.

If-Else Statements

The **if-else** statement is an extension of the basic `if` statement. It allows you to specify an alternative block of code to execute when the condition is false. This gives you more flexibility in making decisions.

Basic Syntax:

cpp

```
if (condition) {
    // Code to execute if the condition is true
} else {
    // Code to execute if the condition is false
}
```

For example:

cpp

```
int age = 16;
if (age >= 18) {
    cout << "You are an adult." << endl;
} else {
    cout << "You are a minor." << endl;
}
```

In this case:

- If `age` is 18 or greater, it will print `"You are an adult."`
- If `age` is less than 18, it will print `"You are a minor."`

How It Works:

- The condition is evaluated first.
- If the condition is **true**, the first block of code executes.
- If the condition is **false**, the program moves to the `else` block and executes that code instead.

Else-If Chains

When you have multiple conditions to check, you can use the `else-if` structure. This allows you to check multiple conditions in sequence and execute the corresponding block of code.

Basic Syntax:
cpp

```
if (condition1) {
    // Code to execute if condition1 is true
} else if (condition2) {
    // Code to execute if condition2 is true
} else if (condition3) {
    // Code to execute if condition3 is true
} else {
    // Code to execute if no condition is true
}
```

For example:

cpp

```
int age = 30;
if (age < 13) {
    cout << "You are a child." << endl;
} else if (age < 18) {
    cout << "You are a teenager." << endl;
} else if (age < 60) {
    cout << "You are an adult." << endl;
} else {
    cout << "You are a senior citizen." << endl;
}
```

Here, the program will check each condition in order:

- If age is less than 13, it prints "You are a child."

- If `age` is between 13 and 17, it prints "`You are a teenager.`"
- If `age` is between 18 and 59, it prints "`You are an adult.`"
- If none of the above conditions is true (i.e., `age` is 60 or older), it prints "`You are a senior citizen.`"

Switch-Case Statements

The `switch-case` statement is another way to make decisions based on different values of a single variable. It is often used when you need to compare one variable against many possible values, making it more efficient than using multiple `if-else` statements.

Basic Syntax:
cpp

```cpp
switch (expression) {
    case value1:
        // Code to execute if expression == value1
        break;
    case value2:
        // Code to execute if expression == value2
        break;
    case value3:
        // Code to execute if expression == value3
        break;
    default:
        // Code to execute if expression doesn't
match any case
}
```

For example:

cpp

```cpp
int day = 3;
switch (day) {
    case 1:
```

```
        cout << "Monday" << endl;
        break;
    case 2:
        cout << "Tuesday" << endl;
        break;
    case 3:
        cout << "Wednesday" << endl;
        break;
    default:
        cout << "Invalid day" << endl;
}
```

In this example:

- If day equals 1, the program prints "Monday".
- If day equals 2, it prints "Tuesday".
- If day equals 3, it prints "Wednesday".
- If day does not match any of the specified cases, the default block executes and prints "Invalid day".

How It Works:

- The switch expression is evaluated once.
- The program then jumps to the case that matches the value of the expression.
- Each case must end with a break statement to stop further execution. Without the break, the program will continue to check subsequent cases even if a match is found.
- The default case is optional but recommended as a fallback for when no cases match.

Logical Operators: and, or, not

Logical operators are used to combine multiple conditions. They allow you to check whether multiple conditions are true or false at the same time. C++ has three primary logical operators:

1. **&& (and):** Returns `true` if **both** conditions are true.
2. **|| (or):** Returns `true` if **at least one** condition is true.
3. **! (not):** Reverses the boolean value of a condition.

Examples:

cpp

```
int age = 25;
bool hasPermission = true;

// Using 'and' (&&)
if (age >= 18 && hasPermission) {
    cout << "You are allowed to enter." << endl;
}

// Using 'or' (||)
if (age < 18 || !hasPermission) {
    cout << "You are not allowed to enter." << endl;
}

// Using 'not' (!)
if (!(age < 18)) {
    cout << "You are an adult." << endl;
}
```

How It Works:

- **&& (and):** In the first `if` statement, the program checks if both `age >= 18` and `hasPermission` are true. Only if both conditions are true will it print `"You are allowed to enter."`
- **|| (or):** In the second `if` statement, the program checks if either `age < 18` **or** `!hasPermission` is true. If either of those is true, it prints `"You are not allowed to enter."`
- **! (not):** In the third `if` statement, the `!` negates the condition `age < 18`, which effectively checks if the user is an adult.

Nested If Statements

A **nested if statement** is simply an `if` statement inside another `if` statement. This is useful when you need to check multiple conditions in a hierarchical manner.

Syntax:

cpp

```cpp
if (condition1) {
    if (condition2) {
        // Code to execute if both conditions are
true
    }
}
```

Example:

cpp

```cpp
int age = 25;
bool hasTicket = true;

if (age >= 18) {
    if (hasTicket) {
        cout << "You are allowed to enter the
concert." << endl;
    } else {
        cout << "You need a ticket to enter." <<
endl;
    }
} else {
    cout << "You must be at least 18 years old to
enter." << endl;
}
```

In this code:

- First, we check if the person is **18 or older.**
- Then, if they are, we check if they **have a ticket** to decide whether they can enter.

How It Works:

- The program first checks `age >= 18`. If the person is old enough, it proceeds to check if they have a ticket.
- If the person is not old enough, it directly prints `"You must be at least 18 years old to enter."`.

Project: Building a Number Guessing Game

Now that we have learned how to control flow in C++ using conditional statements, it's time to apply what we've learned by building a simple **Number Guessing Game**. This game will use **if-else** statements to give feedback to the player based on their guess.

Project Objective:

- The program will generate a random number between 1 and 100.
- The user will input guesses, and the program will tell the player whether the guess is too high, too low, or correct.
- The game will keep running until the player guesses the number correctly.

Code Implementation:
cpp

```cpp
#include <iostream>
#include <cstdlib>
#include <ctime>
using namespace std;

int main() {
    int number, guess;
    int attempts = 0;

    // Seed random number generator
    srand(time(0));
```

```
// Generate random number between 1 and 100
number = rand() % 100 + 1;

cout << "Welcome to the Number Guessing Game!" <<
endl;
cout << "Guess the number between 1 and 100." <<
endl;

do {
    cout << "Enter your guess: ";
    cin >> guess;

    attempts++;

    if (guess > number) {
        cout << "Too high! Try again." << endl;
    } else if (guess < number) {
        cout << "Too low! Try again." << endl;
    } else {
        cout << "Congratulations! You guessed the
number in " << attempts << " attempts." << endl;
    }
} while (guess != number);

return 0;
}
```

Explanation of the Code:

- **Random Number Generation**: We use `rand()` function to generate a random number between 1 and 100. We use `srand(time(0))` to seed the random number generator with the current time, ensuring that we get a different number each time the program is run.
- **User Input**: The program prompts the user to input a guess.
- **Conditional Statements**: Based on whether the guess is too high, too low, or correct, the program provides feedback using `if-else` statements.
- **Looping**: The game continues in a `do-while` loop until the player guesses the correct number.

Conclusion

In this chapter, you have learned how to use **decision-making structures** in C++ to control the flow of your programs. You've gained an understanding of **if statements, if-else** chains, **switch-case** statements, and how to use **logical operators** to combine conditions. Additionally, you learned how to build a fun and practical **Number Guessing Game**, reinforcing the concepts covered in this chapter.

In the next chapter, we will dive deeper into **loops** and **iteration**, where we will explore how to repeat tasks and handle repetitive actions more efficiently in C++. Stay tuned for more exciting projects and hands-on coding!

Chapter 4: Loops and Iteration

Objective:
In this chapter, we will explore **loops** and **iteration techniques** in C++. Loops are fundamental in programming as they allow you to repeat tasks without rewriting code. You'll learn about **for loops, while loops,** and **do-while loops,** including when and how to use each one. By the end of this chapter, you will understand how to control the flow of repetitive tasks and how to apply loops effectively in your programs. As a hands-on exercise, we will create a **Multiplication Table Program**, which will help you reinforce your understanding of loops in a practical, real-world context.

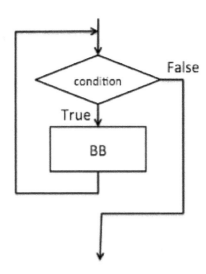

What is a Loop?

A **loop** is a programming concept used to execute a block of code repeatedly based on a condition. Loops are especially useful when you have tasks that need to be repeated multiple times, such as processing items in a list, checking conditions over time, or repeating a calculation. In C++, there are three main types of loops: **for loops, while loops**, and **do-while loops**. Each type of loop serves a specific purpose and is useful in different scenarios.

For Loops: Syntax and Use Cases

A **for loop** is one of the most commonly used loops in C++. It is particularly useful when you know in advance how many times you need to repeat a task. The for loop has three parts:

1. **Initialization**: Where you set up the loop variable.
2. **Condition**: The condition that must be true for the loop to run.
3. **Update**: How the loop variable changes after each iteration.

Basic Syntax:
cpp

```
for (initialization; condition; update) {
    // Code to be executed
}
```

Explanation:

- **Initialization**: This is where you set the starting value of the loop variable. This happens only once, at the start of the loop.
- **Condition**: The loop runs as long as this condition evaluates to `true`. Once the condition evaluates to `false`, the loop stops.

- **Update**: After each iteration, the loop variable is updated (incremented, decremented, or modified in some way).

Example:

cpp

```
#include <iostream>
using namespace std;

int main() {
    // Printing numbers from 1 to 5 using a for loop
    for (int i = 1; i <= 5; i++) {
        cout << i << endl;
    }
    return 0;
}
```

What happens here?

- **Initialization**: `int i = 1;` – We start with `i = 1`.
- **Condition**: `i <= 5` – The loop runs as long as `i` is less than or equal to 5.
- **Update**: `i++` – After each iteration, `i` is incremented by 1.

The output of this loop will be:

```
1
2
3
4
5
```

Common Use Cases for For Loops:

- **Iterating over an array or list**: If you have a collection of items (such as numbers or characters) and need to process each one, a `for loop` is perfect for this task.

- **Repetitive tasks with a known range**: If you know exactly how many times you want the task to repeat, the `for loop` is the best choice.

While Loops: Understanding the Differences and When to Use

A **while loop** is used when you want to repeat a block of code as long as a certain condition is true. The key difference between the `while` loop and the `for` loop is that the `while` loop is generally used when the number of iterations is **not known** ahead of time.

Basic Syntax:
cpp

```
while (condition) {
    // Code to be executed
}
```

Explanation:

- The **condition** is checked before every iteration. If the condition evaluates to `true`, the loop continues to run. If it's `false`, the loop stops.

Example:
cpp

```
#include <iostream>
using namespace std;

int main() {
    int i = 1;
    while (i <= 5) {
        cout << i << endl;
        i++;
    }
    return 0;
```

}

What happens here?

- **Initialization:** `int i = 1;` – We start with `i = 1`.
- **Condition:** `i <= 5` – The loop runs as long as `i` is less than or equal to 5.
- **Update:** `i++` – After each iteration, `i` is incremented by 1.

The output of this loop will be:

```
1
2
3
4
5
```

When to Use While Loops:

- When the number of iterations is **not known** ahead of time.
- When you need to keep asking the user for input until they give a valid response or meet a specific condition (e.g., user authentication).
- In cases where the loop condition is checked at the start, and you need to potentially skip the first iteration or adjust it as the program runs.

Do-While Loops: When to Use Them

A **do-while loop** is very similar to a `while` loop, with the key difference that the condition is checked **after** the loop has executed. This ensures that the loop will run **at least once**, regardless of whether the condition is true or false.

Basic Syntax:

cpp

```
do {
    // Code to be executed
} while (condition);
```

Explanation:

- The code inside the do block will always run at least once before checking the condition.
- After executing the block of code, the program checks the condition. If it evaluates to true, the loop repeats. If it's false, the loop stops.

Example:

cpp

```cpp
#include <iostream>
using namespace std;

int main() {
    int i = 1;
    do {
        cout << i << endl;
        i++;
    } while (i <= 5);
    return 0;
}
```

What happens here?

- The do-while loop executes the code block first, printing 1.
- After the first print, it checks if i <= 5, which is true. The loop runs again, printing 2, and continues until i becomes 6.

The output of this loop will be:

```
1
2
3
4
```

5

- When you want the code to execute **at least once**, regardless of the condition.
- When the loop's condition depends on user input or an external factor that might change after the first iteration.

Nested Loops: Using Loops Inside Loops

You can also **nest** loops within one another. This is useful when dealing with multi-dimensional data, such as creating matrices or iterating through lists of lists. Each loop inside the other is called a **nested loop**.

Example:

cpp

```cpp
#include <iostream>
using namespace std;

int main() {
    for (int i = 1; i <= 3; i++) {
        for (int j = 1; j <= 3; j++) {
            cout << "i = " << i << ", j = " << j <<
endl;
        }
    }
    return 0;
}
```

What happens here?

- The outer loop runs 3 times (for $i = 1$, $i = 2$, and $i = 3$).
- For each iteration of the outer loop, the inner loop runs 3 times, printing the values of i and j.

The output will be:

```ini
i = 1, j = 1
i = 1, j = 2
i = 1, j = 3
i = 2, j = 1
i = 2, j = 2
i = 2, j = 3
i = 3, j = 1
i = 3, j = 2
i = 3, j = 3
```

When to Use Nested Loops:

- When working with multi-dimensional data, like 2D arrays or matrices.
- When you need to repeat a set of tasks within another repetitive task.

Project: Creating a Multiplication Table Program

Now, let's apply what we've learned about loops by creating a **Multiplication Table Program**. This program will take an integer as input and print its multiplication table up to 10.

Project Objective:

- The program will ask the user to input a number.
- It will then display the multiplication table for that number from 1 to 10.

Code Implementation:

cpp

```cpp
#include <iostream>
using namespace std;
```

```cpp
int main() {
    int number;

    // Ask the user to enter a number
    cout << "Enter a number to display its
multiplication table: ";
    cin >> number;

    // Use a for loop to print the multiplication
table
    for (int i = 1; i <= 10; i++) {
        cout << number << " * " << i << " = " <<
number * i << endl;
    }

    return 0;
}
```

Explanation of the Code:

- The program asks the user to input a number.
- It then uses a `for loop` to iterate over numbers 1 through 10.
- Inside the loop, it multiplies the input number by the current loop variable `i` and prints the result.

Sample Output:

css

```
Enter a number to display its multiplication table: 5
5 * 1 = 5
5 * 2 = 10
5 * 3 = 15
5 * 4 = 20
5 * 5 = 25
5 * 6 = 30
5 * 7 = 35
5 * 8 = 40
5 * 9 = 45
5 * 10 = 50
```

Conclusion

In this chapter, you have learned how to use **loops** and iteration techniques in C++ to perform repetitive tasks. We covered:

- **For loops**, which are great when you know exactly how many times you need to repeat a task.
- **While loops**, which are perfect for situations where the number of iterations is not predetermined.
- **Do-while loops**, which ensure that the loop runs at least once before checking the condition.
- **Nested loops**, which allow you to handle more complex repetitive tasks, such as working with multi-dimensional arrays.

As a hands-on project, we built a **Multiplication Table Program** using loops, which helped solidify your understanding of how loops work in real-world applications. In the next chapter, we will explore **functions**, which allow you to write reusable blocks of code, making your programs more modular and easier to manage.

Stay tuned for more coding adventures!

Chapter 5: Functions and Methods

Objective:
In this chapter, we will dive into one of the most powerful features of C++: **functions**. Functions allow you to organize and simplify your code by grouping related tasks into reusable blocks. You'll learn how to define and call functions, pass information to functions using **arguments**, and return results using **return types**. We'll also explore **function overloading**, a useful feature that lets you define multiple functions with the same name. By the end of this chapter, you will understand how to break your programs into modular, manageable pieces, making your code cleaner, easier to debug, and more reusable. We will apply these concepts by building a **temperature converter** that converts temperatures between different units using functions.

What are Functions?

A **function** is a block of code that performs a specific task. Once you define a function, you can "call" it whenever you need that task to be executed. Functions help avoid repetition by letting you write a task once and call it multiple times, making your program easier to manage.

Why Functions?

Functions are a crucial part of structured programming because they:

1. **Simplify code**: Instead of writing the same code multiple times, you write it once in a function and reuse it.
2. **Improve readability**: Functions let you organize your code into logical sections, making it easier to understand.
3. **Allow reusability**: Once written, a function can be called from different parts of the program, reducing redundancy and errors.
4. **Aid debugging**: If there is an error in your program, you only need to troubleshoot the function in which the error occurs, rather than checking all instances of repeated code.

Defining and Calling Functions

In C++, you define a function using the following syntax:

cpp

```
return_type function_name(parameter1, parameter2,
...) {
    // Code to execute
}
```

- `return_type`: This specifies the type of data that the function will return. If the function does not return any data, you use `void`.
- `function_name`: This is the name you give to your function. It should describe the task the function performs.
- `parameter1, parameter2, ...`: These are inputs that you pass into the function. Functions can accept multiple parameters (or none), depending on the task.

Example:
cpp

```
#include <iostream>
using namespace std;
```

```
void sayHello() {
    cout << "Hello, World!" << endl;
}

int main() {
    // Calling the function
    sayHello();
    return 0;
}
```

- The function `sayHello()` is defined with the return type `void` because it does not return any value.
- Inside the `main()` function, we call `sayHello()` to execute the code within it, which prints `"Hello, World!"`.

How It Works:

1. **Function Definition**: We define the function `sayHello()`, which contains the block of code to be executed.
2. **Function Call**: We call the function inside the `main()` function by writing `sayHello();`. The program jumps to the function, executes its code, and then returns to the point where the function was called.

Function Arguments and Return Types

A function can also accept **arguments**, which are values or variables passed into the function when it is called. Additionally, a function can **return** a value, which is the result of its execution.

Function Arguments (Parameters)

You can define functions that accept **inputs** (arguments) that are used within the function. For example, if you need a function to add two numbers, you would pass the numbers as arguments to that function.

cpp

```cpp
#include <iostream>
using namespace std;

// Function that adds two numbers and returns the
result
int addNumbers(int a, int b) {
    return a + b;
}

int main() {
    int result = addNumbers(5, 3); // Pass values to
the function
    cout << "The sum is: " << result << endl;
    return 0;
}
```

In this code:

- The function `addNumbers()` takes two parameters, `a` and `b`, both of type `int`.
- The function adds `a` and `b` and returns the result.
- In `main()`, we call `addNumbers()` with the arguments 5 and 3 and store the result in the `result` variable.

Return Types

The **return type** of a function specifies what type of value (if any) the function will return. A function can return different types of values, such as integers (`int`), floating-point numbers (`double`), or even strings (`string`).

- If a function does not need to return a value, we use the `void` return type.

- If a function returns a value, we specify the type of that value in the function's definition.

<u>Example with Return Type:</u>
cpp

```cpp
#include <iostream>
using namespace std;

double multiply(double x, double y) {
    return x * y;
}

int main() {
    double result = multiply(4.5, 2.0);
    cout << "The product is: " << result << endl;
    return 0;
}
```

In this example:

- `multiply()` takes two `double` parameters (x and y) and returns their product.
- The return type `double` is specified because the result of multiplying two `double` values is also a `double`.

Function Overloading: Understanding Multiple Functions with the Same Name

Function overloading allows you to define multiple functions with the same name, but with different parameters. C++ uses the number and type of parameters to differentiate between overloaded functions. This is useful when you want to perform the same task but with different types or numbers of inputs.

Example:

cpp

```cpp
#include <iostream>
using namespace std;

// Function to add two integers
int add(int a, int b) {
    return a + b;
}

// Function to add two doubles
double add(double a, double b) {
    return a + b;
}

int main() {
    cout << "Sum of integers: " << add(3, 4) << endl;
    cout << "Sum of doubles: " << add(3.5, 4.5) <<
endl;
    return 0;
}
```

In this example:

- We have two add() functions, one for adding integers and another for adding doubles.
- C++ automatically selects the correct function based on the types of arguments passed during the call.

How It Works:

- **First Function:** add(int a, int b) accepts two integers.
- **Second Function:** add(double a, double b) accepts two doubles.
- When we call add(3, 4), C++ uses the integer version of add(), and when we call add(3.5, 4.5), C++ uses the double version.

When to Use Function Overloading:

- When the function name describes the same task but the inputs vary in type or number.
- For example, functions that perform mathematical operations can be overloaded to handle different types of numbers, like `int`, `double`, or `float`.

Project: Build a Temperature Converter Using Functions

Now that you understand functions and their power in simplifying your code, let's apply what we've learned by building a **Temperature Converter**. The program will allow the user to convert temperatures between **Celsius** and **Fahrenheit** using functions.

Project Objective:

- The program will ask the user for a temperature value and the unit (Celsius or Fahrenheit).
- It will then convert the temperature to the other unit.
- We will use functions to perform the conversion and ensure the program is modular.

Code Implementation:

cpp

```cpp
#include <iostream>
using namespace std;

// Function to convert Celsius to Fahrenheit
double celsiusToFahrenheit(double celsius) {
    return (celsius * 9 / 5) + 32;
}

// Function to convert Fahrenheit to Celsius
```

```
double fahrenheitToCelsius(double fahrenheit) {
    return (fahrenheit - 32) * 5 / 9;
}

int main() {
    double temperature;
    char unit;

    cout << "Enter the temperature value: ";
    cin >> temperature;
    cout << "Enter the unit (C for Celsius, F for
Fahrenheit): ";
    cin >> unit;

    if (unit == 'C' || unit == 'c') {
        double fahrenheit =
celsiusToFahrenheit(temperature);
        cout << temperature << " Celsius is equal to
" << fahrenheit << " Fahrenheit." << endl;
    } else if (unit == 'F' || unit == 'f') {
        double celsius =
fahrenheitToCelsius(temperature);
        cout << temperature << " Fahrenheit is equal
to " << celsius << " Celsius." << endl;
    } else {
        cout << "Invalid unit!" << endl;
    }

    return 0;
}
```

Explanation of the Code:

- **celsiusToFahrenheit()**: This function takes a temperature in Celsius as an argument and converts it to Fahrenheit using the formula `(Celsius * 9 / 5) + 32`.
- **fahrenheitToCelsius()**: This function takes a temperature in Fahrenheit and converts it to Celsius using the formula `(Fahrenheit - 32) * 5 / 9`.
- **In the main() function:**
  - We ask the user to input a temperature and the unit (C or F).

- o Based on the user's choice of unit, we call the appropriate function to convert the temperature.

Sample Output:

```
mathematica
```

```
Enter the temperature value: 100
Enter the unit (C for Celsius, F for Fahrenheit): C
100 Celsius is equal to 212 Fahrenheit.
```

How It Works:

1. The user inputs a temperature and a unit.
2. The program calls either `celsiusToFahrenheit()` or `fahrenheitToCelsius()` based on the user's input.
3. The appropriate conversion function is called, and the result is displayed to the user.

Conclusion

In this chapter, we explored the concept of **functions** in C++, which allows us to modularize our code by grouping related tasks into reusable blocks. We covered:

- **Defining and calling functions**, which allow you to execute specific tasks in different parts of your program.
- **Function arguments and return types**, showing how to pass data into functions and get results back.
- **Function overloading**, which enables you to create multiple functions with the same name but different parameters.
- We applied these concepts in the creation of a **Temperature Converter**, which demonstrated how functions can simplify your code and make it more modular.

In the next chapter, we will take a deeper look at **arrays**, which allow you to store and manipulate multiple values in a single data structure. Stay tuned as we continue to build more practical programs!

Chapter 6: Arrays and Strings

Objective:
In this chapter, we'll delve into two powerful features in C++: **arrays** and **strings**. Both allow you to work with collections of data, making it easier to store and manipulate multiple values in a single variable. Arrays are great for storing a fixed number of values, while strings are specialized arrays that deal with text. By the end of this chapter, you'll understand how to **declare and use arrays**, explore **multidimensional arrays** (arrays of arrays), and work with **strings** in C++. You'll also apply your knowledge by creating a **Student Gradebook Program** that will store student grades using arrays and allow you to perform basic operations on them.

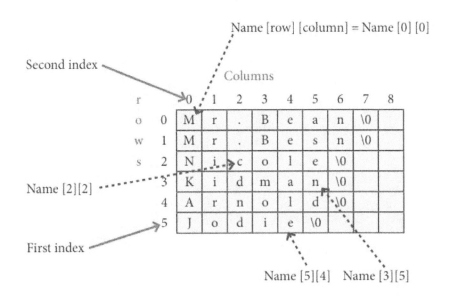

What are Arrays?

An **array** is a collection of variables of the **same type** that are stored in contiguous memory locations. Arrays allow you to store multiple values under a single variable name, making it easier to work with groups of data.

Why Use Arrays?

Arrays are useful when:

- You have a known number of elements to store.
- You want to process multiple items in a consistent manner.
- You need to efficiently access elements by index.

Declaring and Using Arrays

To declare an array in C++, you specify:

1. The type of elements the array will hold (e.g., `int`, `double`, `char`).
2. The name of the array.
3. The number of elements the array can hold (this is known as the **size**).

Basic Syntax:
cpp

```
type array_name[size];
```

- **type**: The data type of the elements (e.g., `int`, `double`).
- **array_name**: The name you want to give to the array.
- **size**: The number of elements the array can hold.

Example:

cpp

```cpp
#include <iostream>
using namespace std;

int main() {
    int scores[5]; // Declare an array of 5 integers

    // Assign values to the array elements
    scores[0] = 85;
    scores[1] = 90;
    scores[2] = 78;
    scores[3] = 92;
    scores[4] = 88;

    // Access and display array elements
    cout << "Score of student 1: " << scores[0] <<
endl;
    cout << "Score of student 2: " << scores[1] <<
endl;

    return 0;
}
```

Explanation:

- The array scores can hold 5 integers. The elements are indexed from 0 to 4.
- We assign values to each element of the array using the index notation, such as scores[0] = 85.
- We can access and print individual elements using the index, like scores[0].

Array Indexing:

Arrays in C++ are **zero-indexed**, meaning the first element is accessed with index 0, the second element with index 1, and so on.

Multidimensional Arrays: Arrays of Arrays

In C++, you can create **multidimensional arrays**. These are arrays that contain other arrays. They are useful when dealing with tables, grids, or matrices, where data is organized into rows and columns.

Declaring a Multidimensional Array

A **two-dimensional array** is the most common form of multidimensional array. It's essentially an array of arrays. Here's the syntax for declaring a 2D array:

cpp

```
type array_name[row_size][column_size];
```

- **`row_size`**: The number of rows in the array.
- **`column_size`**: The number of columns in each row.

Example:

cpp

```
#include <iostream>
using namespace std;

int main() {
    // Declare a 2D array with 3 rows and 4 columns
    int matrix[3][4] = {
        {1, 2, 3, 4},
        {5, 6, 7, 8},
        {9, 10, 11, 12}
    };

    // Access and display elements from the 2D array
    cout << "Element at (1,2): " << matrix[1][2] <<
endl; // Accessing element in 2nd row, 3rd column
    cout << "Element at (2,4): " << matrix[2][3] <<
endl; // Accessing element in 3rd row, 4th column

    return 0;
```

```
}
```

Explanation:

- The 2D array `matrix[3][4]` is a 3-row by 4-column matrix.
- Each element in the matrix is accessed using two indices: the first for the row, and the second for the column.
- For example, `matrix[1][2]` accesses the element in the second row and third column.

Accessing 2D Array Elements:

To access an element in a 2D array, you specify the row and column indices:

- `matrix[row][column]`
- Keep in mind that arrays are zero-indexed, so the first row is `0`, the second row is `1`, and so on.

C++ Strings and String Functions

In C++, a **string** is a sequence of characters. Unlike arrays, strings are designed specifically to handle text. While arrays can be used to store characters, the `string` type provides a more convenient way to manipulate text.

Declaring and Using Strings

In C++, strings are part of the **Standard Library**, and the `string` type is defined within the `std` namespace. To declare a string, you can use the following syntax:

```cpp
cpp
```

```cpp
string str;
```

You can initialize the string directly by assigning a value to it:

cpp

```
string name = "John Doe";
```

Example:
cpp

```
#include <iostream>
#include <string> // Include the string library
using namespace std;

int main() {
    string name = "Alice";
    string greeting = "Hello, ";

    // Concatenate strings
    string message = greeting + name; // "Hello,
Alice"

    cout << message << endl; // Output: Hello, Alice
    return 0;
}
```

Explanation:

- The + operator is used to **concatenate** two strings, combining "Hello, " with "Alice", resulting in "Hello, Alice".

Common String Functions:

C++ provides a wide range of functions to manipulate strings:

- **length()**: Returns the number of characters in the string.
- **substr()**: Extracts a substring from a string.
- **find()**: Searches for a substring within a string.
- **append()**: Adds characters to the end of the string.

Example with String Functions:

cpp

```cpp
#include <iostream>
#include <string>
using namespace std;

int main() {
    string message = "Hello, World!";

    // Getting the length of the string
    cout << "Length of message: " << message.length()
<< endl; // Output: 13

    // Extracting a substring
    string sub = message.substr(7, 5); // Extract
"World"
    cout << "Substring: " << sub << endl; // Output:
World

    // Finding a substring
    size_t position = message.find("World");
    if (position != string::npos) {
        cout << "'World' found at position: " <<
position << endl; // Output: 7
    }

    return 0;
}
```

Explanation:

- **length()** returns the number of characters in the string `"Hello, World!"`.
- **substr(7, 5)** extracts the substring starting from index 7 and with a length of 5 characters, resulting in `"World"`.
- **find("World")** finds the position of the substring `"World"` within the string.

Project: Creating a Student Gradebook with Arrays

Now that we've covered arrays and strings, let's apply these concepts in a **Student Gradebook Program**. This program will allow you to store student grades in an array, and you can perform operations like calculating the average grade, finding the highest grade, and more.

Project Objective:

- The program will store grades for multiple students using an array.
- It will calculate the average grade of the class.
- It will print the highest and lowest grades.
- It will also allow the user to input new grades and update the gradebook.

Code Implementation:
cpp

```cpp
#include <iostream>
#include <string>
using namespace std;

int main() {
    const int numStudents = 5;
    int grades[numStudents];
    string students[numStudents] = {"Alice", "Bob",
"Charlie", "David", "Eva"};

    // Input grades
    for (int i = 0; i < numStudents; i++) {
        cout << "Enter grade for " << students[i] <<
": ";
        cin >> grades[i];
    }
```

```cpp
    // Calculate the average grade
    int total = 0;
    for (int i = 0; i < numStudents; i++) {
        total += grades[i];
    }
    double average = total /
static_cast<double>(numStudents);
    cout << "Average grade: " << average << endl;

    // Find the highest and lowest grades
    int highest = grades[0], lowest = grades[0];
    for (int i = 1; i < numStudents; i++) {
        if (grades[i] > highest) {
            highest = grades[i];
        }
        if (grades[i] < lowest) {
            lowest = grades[i];
        }
    }
    cout << "Highest grade: " << highest << endl;
    cout << "Lowest grade: " << lowest << endl;

    return 0;
}
```

Explanation of the Code:

- **Array for Grades:** `int grades[numStudents]` stores the grades of 5 students.
- **Array for Student Names:** `string students[numStudents]` stores the names of the students.
- **Input:** The program prompts the user to input grades for each student using a `for` loop.
- **Average Calculation:** The program calculates the average by summing up all the grades and dividing by the number of students.
- **Highest and Lowest Grades:** The program uses a `for` loop to compare each grade and find the highest and lowest values.

Sample Output:

```yaml
yaml

Enter grade for Alice: 90
Enter grade for Bob: 85
Enter grade for Charlie: 95
Enter grade for David: 80
Enter grade for Eva: 88
Average grade: 87.6
Highest grade: 95
Lowest grade: 80
```

Conclusion

In this chapter, you learned how to work with **arrays** and **strings** in C++. We covered:

- **Arrays**: How to store and manipulate multiple values of the same type.
- **Multidimensional Arrays**: How to work with more complex data structures like matrices.
- **Strings**: How to handle text data and manipulate it using built-in functions.
- We applied this knowledge in the creation of a **Student Gradebook Program**, which demonstrated how arrays and strings can be used in practical applications.

In the next chapter, we will explore **pointers and memory management**, which will allow you to gain finer control over memory allocation and improve the performance of your programs. Stay tuned for more advanced C++ topics!

Chapter 7: Pointers and Memory Management

Objective:
In this chapter, we will introduce **pointers** and **memory management** in C++, two crucial concepts that allow you to efficiently manage and manipulate memory in your programs. You'll learn what pointers are, how to use them with **dereferencing** and **pointer arithmetic**, and understand **dynamic memory allocation**, which allows you to allocate memory during runtime. You will apply these concepts in the project to build a **simple linked list using pointers**, which is a common data structure used to store and manipulate collections of data.

What Are Pointers?

A **pointer** in C++ is a variable that holds the **memory address** of another variable. In simple terms, instead of holding a value like a normal variable, a pointer holds the location in memory where the value is stored. Pointers allow you to work directly with memory, which can make your programs more efficient and flexible.

Why Pointers?

Pointers are powerful tools in C++ for the following reasons:

1. **Efficiency**: Pointers allow you to work with large data structures or arrays efficiently without ing data.
2. **Dynamic Memory Allocation**: With pointers, you can allocate memory at runtime, which is crucial for programs that handle a variable amount of data.

3. **Direct Memory Access**: Pointers provide the ability to manipulate memory directly, which is helpful for performance optimizations.

Declaring and Initializing Pointers

A pointer is declared using the * operator. The * indicates that the variable is a pointer, and it tells C++ that the variable will store a memory address rather than a direct value.

cpp

```
type* pointer_name;
```

For example:

cpp

```
int* ptr;
```

This declares a pointer ptr that can point to an integer.

To initialize a pointer, you assign it the **memory address** of a variable using the address-of operator &.

cpp

```
int num = 5;
int* ptr = &num; // ptr now holds the address of num
```

Here:

- num is a regular integer variable with a value of 5.
- ptr is a pointer that stores the **memory address** of num.

Pointer Syntax Breakdown:

- **& (Address-of Operator)**: The & operator gives the memory address of a variable.
  - For example, `ptr = &num;` stores the address of `num` in `ptr`.
- *** (Dereferencing Operator)**: The * operator is used to access the value stored at the memory address that the pointer is pointing to. This is called **dereferencing** the pointer.
  - For example, `cout << *ptr;` will print the value of `num` because `ptr` points to `num`.

Example:

cpp

```
#include <iostream>
using namespace std;

int main() {
    int num = 10;
    int* ptr = &num; // ptr points to num

    cout << "Address of num: " << &num << endl;
    cout << "Address stored in ptr: " << ptr << endl;
    cout << "Value of num via ptr: " << *ptr << endl;

    return 0;
}
```

Output:

yaml

```
Address of num: 0x7fffdde12345
Address stored in ptr: 0x7fffdde12345
Value of num via ptr: 10
```

In this example:

- `&num` gives the memory address of the variable `num`.
- `ptr` holds the memory address of `num`.
- `*ptr` dereferences the pointer to get the value stored at the address, which is `10`.

Dereferencing and Pointer Arithmetic

Dereferencing Pointers

Dereferencing is the process of accessing the value stored at the memory address a pointer is pointing to. You use the `*` operator to dereference a pointer.

cpp

```
int num = 20;
int* ptr = &num;   // ptr holds the address of num

cout << *ptr;   // Dereferencing ptr to print the
value stored at the address (20)
```

Pointer Arithmetic

C++ allows you to perform arithmetic operations on pointers, which is particularly useful when working with arrays or dynamic memory. When you increment a pointer, it moves to the next memory location based on the type of data the pointer is pointing to.

For example, if you have a pointer to an integer, incrementing the pointer moves it by the size of an integer (usually 4 bytes on most systems).

cpp

```
int arr[] = {10, 20, 30};
int* ptr = arr;   // Pointer to the first element of
the array
```

```
cout << *ptr << endl;   // Prints 10

ptr++;   // Moves to the next element (increments by
the size of an integer)

cout << *ptr << endl;   // Prints 20
```

Here, `ptr++` moves the pointer to the next integer in the array. Each time you increment the pointer, it moves by the size of the data type it points to (in this case, 4 bytes for `int`).

Dynamic Memory Allocation

Dynamic memory allocation is the process of allocating memory at runtime using pointers. Unlike static memory allocation, where the memory size is defined at compile-time, dynamic memory allocation allows you to allocate memory during the program's execution, which is especially useful for handling data whose size may change.

Using `new` and `delete` for Dynamic Memory Allocation

In C++, the `new` operator is used to allocate memory dynamically, while the `delete` operator is used to free that memory when it is no longer needed.

- **new**: Allocates memory on the heap and returns a pointer to it.
- **delete**: Deallocates memory that was previously allocated using `new`.

Example of Dynamic Memory Allocation:
cpp

```
#include <iostream>
using namespace std;
```

```
int main() {
    // Dynamically allocate memory for an integer
    int* ptr = new int;
    *ptr = 42;   // Assign value to the allocated
memory

    cout << "Dynamically allocated value: " << *ptr
<< endl;

    // Free dynamically allocated memory
    delete ptr;

    return 0;
}
```

Explanation:

- `new int` dynamically allocates memory to store an integer on the heap and returns a pointer to it.
- We assign the value `42` to the allocated memory using `*ptr`.
- Finally, `delete ptr` deallocates the memory, preventing memory leaks.

Dynamic Arrays

You can also use `new` to allocate memory for arrays dynamically. This allows you to allocate memory for arrays whose size is determined at runtime.

cpp

```
#include <iostream>
using namespace std;

int main() {
    int size;
    cout << "Enter size of array: ";
    cin >> size;

    // Dynamically allocate memory for an array of
integers
```

```
int* arr = new int[size];

// Assign values to the array
for (int i = 0; i < size; i++) {
    arr[i] = i + 1;
}

// Display the array
for (int i = 0; i < size; i++) {
    cout << arr[i] << " ";
}

// Free dynamically allocated memory
delete[] arr;

return 0;
}
```

Explanation:

- `new int[size]` dynamically allocates an array of integers, where `size` is determined by the user at runtime.
- The program assigns values to the array and prints them.
- Finally, `delete[] arr` frees the memory allocated for the array.

Project: Building a Simple Linked List with Pointers

Now that you've learned about pointers and memory management, let's apply these concepts by creating a **linked list**. A linked list is a data structure in which each element (called a "node") contains data and a pointer to the next node in the list. Unlike arrays, linked lists do not require contiguous memory and can grow or shrink dynamically.

Project Objective:

- We will create a **simple singly linked list** to store student names.

- Each node will contain a student's name and a pointer to the next node.
- The program will allow you to add new students to the list and display all the students.

Code Implementation:

cpp

```cpp
#include <iostream>
using namespace std;

// Node structure representing each student
struct Node {
    string name;      // Student's name
    Node* next;       // Pointer to the next node

    // Constructor to initialize node
    Node(string name) : name(name), next(nullptr) {}
};

// Function to add a student to the list
void addStudent(Node*& head, const string& name) {
    Node* newNode = new Node(name);
    newNode->next = head;   // New node points to the
current head
    head = newNode;         // New node becomes the
head of the list
}

// Function to display the list of students
void displayStudents(Node* head) {
    Node* current = head;
    while (current != nullptr) {
        cout << current->name << endl;
        current = current->next;
    }
}

int main() {
    Node* head = nullptr;   // Initialize an empty
list

    // Add students to the list
```

```
addStudent(head, "Alice");
addStudent(head, "Bob");
addStudent(head, "Charlie");

// Display the students
cout << "Student List:" << endl;
displayStudents(head);

// Free dynamically allocated memory
Node* current = head;
while (current != nullptr) {
    Node* temp = current;
    current = current->next;
    delete temp;
}

return 0;
}
```

Explanation of the Code:

- **Node Structure**: The `Node` structure contains two fields:
  - `name`: A string holding the student's name.
  - `next`: A pointer to the next `Node` in the list.
- **addStudent Function**: This function adds a new student to the beginning of the list. It dynamically creates a new node, sets its `next` pointer to the current head, and then updates the head to point to the new node.
- **displayStudents Function**: This function traverses the linked list, starting from the head, and prints each student's name.
- **Memory Management**: The program frees the dynamically allocated memory for each node using `delete` to avoid memory leaks.

Sample Output:

yaml

```
Student List:
Charlie
```

```
Bob
Alice
```

In this program:

- The students are added to the list in reverse order (since we add each new student at the beginning of the list).
- After displaying the list, the memory allocated for each node is freed.

Conclusion

In this chapter, we explored the power of **pointers** and **memory management** in C++. We covered:

- **Pointers**: Understanding how to use pointers to store memory addresses and manipulate data directly.
- **Dereferencing and Pointer Arithmetic**: How to access and modify the data pointed to by a pointer, and how to perform arithmetic on pointers.
- **Dynamic Memory Allocation**: How to allocate and deallocate memory during runtime using `new` and `delete`.
- We applied these concepts by building a **linked list**, which demonstrated how to manage dynamic data efficiently using pointers.

Chapter 8: Object-Oriented Programming (OOP) Basics

Objective:
In this chapter, we will introduce the fundamentals of **Object-Oriented Programming (OOP)** in C++, a core programming paradigm that helps you structure your programs in a more modular, flexible, and reusable way. You'll learn key concepts like **classes, objects, encapsulation, constructors**, and **destructors**. Through these concepts, you'll understand how to design and build complex systems more efficiently. As a practical application, we'll walk through designing a class for a **Bank Account system**, demonstrating how to use OOP principles to model real-world entities.

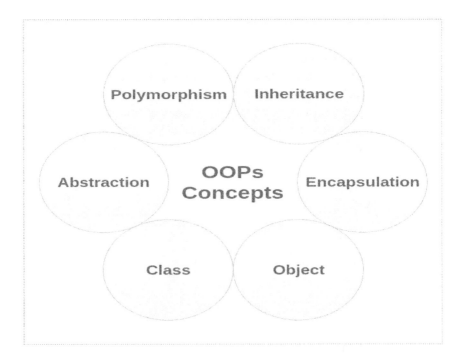

What is Object-Oriented Programming (OOP)?

Object-Oriented Programming is a programming paradigm that organizes software design around **objects** rather than functions and logic. These objects can represent real-world entities and behaviors. The core idea of OOP is to bundle related properties (data) and methods (functions) into a single unit, called a **class**.

Key Principles of OOP:

1. **Encapsulation**: Hiding the internal workings of an object and exposing only what is necessary.
2. **Inheritance**: Creating a new class from an existing class, inheriting its properties and behaviors.
3. **Polymorphism**: Allowing different classes to be treated as instances of the same class through a common interface.
4. **Abstraction**: Hiding complex implementation details and exposing only the essential features.

In C++, classes and objects are the primary mechanisms for implementing OOP. Let's dive deeper into **classes** and **objects**.

Classes and Objects

A **class** is a blueprint for creating **objects**. An object is an instance of a class. A class defines the properties (data) and methods (functions) that objects of that class will have.

Declaring a Class:

Here is the basic syntax for declaring a class in C++:

cpp

```
class ClassName {
    // Data members (attributes)
    private:
        type member_variable;

    // Member functions (methods)
    public:
        return_type function_name(parameters) {
            // Function body
        }
};
```

- **Data Members**: These are the attributes or properties that define the state of an object.
- **Member Functions**: These are the behaviors or methods that an object can perform.
- **Access Specifiers**: These determine the accessibility of the members of the class. The most common access specifiers are:
    - `public`: Members are accessible from anywhere in the program.
    - `private`: Members are only accessible from within the class itself.
    - `protected`: Members are accessible within the class and by derived classes.

Example:
cpp

```
#include <iostream>
using namespace std;

class Car {
    private:
        string make;
        string model;

    public:
        // Constructor
        Car(string m, string mod) {
```

```
            make = m;
            model = mod;
        }

        // Method to display car details
        void displayDetails() {
            cout << "Car Make: " << make << endl;
            cout << "Car Model: " << model << endl;
        }
};

int main() {
    // Creating an object of the Car class
    Car car1("Toyota", "Corolla");
    car1.displayDetails();  // Calling the method to
display details

    return 0;
}
```

Explanation:

- **Car Class**: The class has two private data members `make`
  and `model` and one public method `displayDetails()`.
- **Constructor**: The constructor `Car(string m, string
  mod)` initializes the `make` and `model` of the car when an
  object is created.
- **Object Creation**: In `main()`, an object `car1` of type `Car` is
  created and initialized with `"Toyota"` and `"Corolla"`.

Encapsulation: Private and Public Members

Encapsulation is the concept of bundling the data (attributes) and
the methods (functions) that operate on the data into a single unit, a
class. It also involves restricting access to certain components of an
object and only exposing what is necessary for interacting with the
object.

Private and Public Members

- **Private Members**: These are attributes and methods that can only be accessed within the class. They cannot be accessed directly from outside the class.
- **Public Members**: These are attributes and methods that can be accessed from outside the class.

This is the concept of **data hiding**, where the internal state of an object is hidden from the outside world, and access is provided through **getter** and **setter** functions.

Example:

cpp

```cpp
#include <iostream>
using namespace std;

class BankAccount {
    private:
        double balance;

    public:
        // Constructor to initialize balance
        BankAccount(double initialBalance) {
            if (initialBalance >= 0) {
                balance = initialBalance;
            } else {
                balance = 0;
            }
        }

        // Getter method to access balance
        double getBalance() {
            return balance;
        }

        // Setter method to modify balance
        void deposit(double amount) {
            if (amount > 0) {
                balance += amount;
```

```
            }
        }

        void withdraw(double amount) {
            if (amount > 0 && amount <= balance) {
                balance -= amount;
            } else {
                cout << "Invalid withdrawal amount!"
<< endl;
            }
        }
};

int main() {
    BankAccount account(1000);   // Create an account
with initial balance of 1000

    account.deposit(500);   // Deposit 500
    cout << "Balance after deposit: " <<
account.getBalance() << endl;

    account.withdraw(300);   // Withdraw 300
    cout << "Balance after withdrawal: " <<
account.getBalance() << endl;

    account.withdraw(1500);   // Attempt to withdraw
more than the balance
    cout << "Balance after invalid withdrawal: " <<
account.getBalance() << endl;

    return 0;
}
```

Explanation:

- **Private Member `balance`:** The `balance` of the bank account is a private member, so it cannot be accessed directly from outside the class.
- **Getter and Setter Methods:** `getBalance()` and `deposit()`/`withdraw()` are public methods that provide controlled access to the private `balance` member.

- **Constructor:** The constructor initializes the `balance` when a `BankAccount` object is created.

Constructors and Destructors

In C++, **constructors** and **destructors** are special types of member functions used for initializing and cleaning up objects.

Constructors

A **constructor** is a special function that is automatically called when an object is created. It is used to initialize the object's attributes. Constructors have the same name as the class and do not have a return type.

- **Default Constructor:** A constructor that takes no arguments.
- **Parameterized Constructor:** A constructor that takes arguments to initialize the object with specific values.

Example:
cpp

```cpp
class Rectangle {
    private:
        double length;
        double width;

    public:
        // Default constructor
        Rectangle() {
            length = 0;
            width = 0;
        }

        // Parameterized constructor
        Rectangle(double l, double w) {
```

```
            length = l;
            width = w;
        }

        double area() {
            return length * width;
        }
};
```

In the above example:

- The **default constructor** initializes the rectangle with length
  and width as 0.
- The **parameterized constructor** allows you to create a
  rectangle with specific dimensions.

Destructors

A **destructor** is a special function that is automatically called when
an object is destroyed. Destructors are typically used for cleaning up
any dynamically allocated memory or resources that the object
used. The destructor has the same name as the class, preceded by a
tilde (~), and it does not take any parameters or return anything.

cpp

```
class MyClass {
    public:
        MyClass() {
            cout << "Constructor called" << endl;
        }

        ~MyClass() {
            cout << "Destructor called" << endl;
        }
};

int main() {
    MyClass obj;  // Constructor is called when the
object is created
```

```cpp
    // Destructor will be called automatically when
the object goes out of scope
    return 0;
}
```

In this example:

- The **constructor** prints a message when an object is created.
- The **destructor** prints a message when the object is destroyed, which happens automatically when it goes out of scope.

Project: Designing a Class for a Bank Account System

Let's put everything we've learned into practice by designing a simple **Bank Account System** using a class. This system will allow users to create an account, deposit money, withdraw money, and check their balance.

Project Objective:

- Create a class `BankAccount` with attributes for the account holder's name and balance.
- Include methods for depositing, withdrawing, and checking the balance.
- Implement a constructor to initialize the account with the holder's name and initial balance.
- Implement a destructor to print a message when the account is destroyed.

Code Implementation:
cpp

```cpp
#include <iostream>
#include <string>
```

```cpp
using namespace std;

class BankAccount {
    private:
        string holderName;
        double balance;

    public:
        // Constructor
        BankAccount(string name, double
initialBalance) {
            holderName = name;
            if (initialBalance >= 0) {
                balance = initialBalance;
            } else {
                balance = 0;
            }
        }

        // Destructor
        ~BankAccount() {
            cout << "Bank account for " << holderName
<< " is closed." << endl;
        }

        // Deposit method
        void deposit(double amount) {
            if (amount > 0) {
                balance += amount;
                cout << amount << " deposited. New
balance: " << balance << endl;
            } else {
                cout << "Deposit amount must be
positive." << endl;
            }
        }

        // Withdraw method
        void withdraw(double amount) {
            if (amount <= balance && amount > 0) {
                balance -= amount;
                cout << amount << " withdrawn. New
balance: " << balance << endl;
            } else {
```

```
                cout << "Invalid withdrawal amount."
<< endl;
            }
        }

        // Get the balance
        double getBalance() {
            return balance;
        }

        // Display account details
        void displayAccountDetails() {
            cout << "Account holder: " << holderName
<< endl;
            cout << "Balance: " << balance << endl;
        }
};

int main() {
    // Creating a bank account
    BankAccount account("John Doe", 500.00);

    // Displaying account details
    account.displayAccountDetails();

    // Depositing money
    account.deposit(200);

    // Withdrawing money
    account.withdraw(100);

    // Displaying final balance
    cout << "Final balance: " << account.getBalance()
<< endl;

    return 0;
}
```

Explanation of the Code:

- **BankAccount Class:**

- ○ **Attributes:** `holderName` and `balance` are private attributes that store the account holder's name and the account balance.
- ○ **Constructor:** The constructor takes the account holder's name and initial balance and initializes the account.
- ○ **Methods:**
  - `deposit()`: Deposits a specified amount into the account.
  - `withdraw()`: Withdraws a specified amount, checking if there are enough funds.
  - `getBalance()`: Returns the current balance.
  - `displayAccountDetails()`: Displays the account holder's name and balance.
- ○ **Destructor:** Prints a message when the account is closed (i.e., when the object is destroyed).

Conclusion

In this chapter, we introduced the foundational concepts of **Object-Oriented Programming (OOP)** in C++. These concepts are essential for structuring your programs in a modular, maintainable way. We covered:

- **Classes and Objects**: How to define and create objects using classes.
- **Encapsulation**: How to protect the internal state of an object by making some members private and providing access through public methods.
- **Constructors and Destructors**: How constructors initialize objects and how destructors clean up when objects are destroyed.
- We applied these concepts in a **Bank Account System**, demonstrating how to model real-world entities using classes.

In the next chapter, we will dive deeper into more advanced OOP concepts, such as **inheritance** and **polymorphism,** which allow you to create more complex systems and build upon existing code. Stay tuned as we continue our journey through C++ programming!

Chapter 9: Advanced Object-Oriented Programming (OOP) Concepts

Objective:
In this chapter, we will explore more advanced principles of **Object-Oriented Programming (OOP)** in C++. These advanced concepts will allow you to write more efficient, modular, and scalable code. Specifically, we will dive into **inheritance**, **polymorphism**, and **abstraction**, three key principles of OOP that allow you to extend and manipulate your code in powerful ways. Through these concepts, you'll learn how to create more flexible and maintainable programs. To bring these principles to life, we will apply them in a **project**: building an **Inventory Management System** using inheritance.

What Are Advanced OOP Concepts?

At its core, Object-Oriented Programming revolves around creating **objects** that encapsulate data and behavior. While the basic OOP principles (like classes, objects, and encapsulation) give you a foundation for writing object-oriented code, **advanced OOP concepts** like inheritance, polymorphism, and abstraction provide the tools to build more complex systems.

These principles allow you to:

- Reuse existing code (inheritance).
- Create flexible code that can handle new types of objects (polymorphism).
- Hide unnecessary details and expose only the essential features of a system (abstraction).

In this chapter, we will break down each of these principles and explain how to apply them in real-world applications.

Inheritance and Derived Classes

Inheritance is one of the key principles of OOP that allows a class to inherit the properties and methods of another class. The class that is inherited from is called the **base class** (or parent class), and the class that inherits is called the **derived class** (or child class). Inheritance allows you to reuse code from the base class and extend or modify it in the derived class.

Why Use Inheritance?

1. **Code Reusability**: Instead of rewriting common functionality, you can inherit it from an existing class.
2. **Extensibility**: You can extend the functionality of a class without modifying the original class, making your program more flexible.

Basic Syntax for Inheritance:

cpp

```cpp
class BaseClass {
    // Base class code
};

class DerivedClass : public BaseClass {
    // Derived class code
};
```

- **public**: This is the most common access specifier for inheritance. It means that all **public** and **protected** members of the base class are inherited as public or protected members in the derived class.
- **protected** and **private** inheritance are also possible but less common. They restrict the accessibility of inherited members.

Example:

cpp

```cpp
#include <iostream>
using namespace std;

// Base class
class Animal {
public:
    void eat() {
        cout << "Eating..." << endl;
    }
};

// Derived class
class Dog : public Animal {
public:
    void bark() {
        cout << "Barking..." << endl;
    }
};

int main() {
    Dog myDog;
    myDog.eat();  // Inherited from Animal class
    myDog.bark(); // Defined in Dog class

    return 0;
}
```

In this example:

- The class `Dog` **inherits** the `eat()` method from the `Animal` class, so objects of `Dog` can use this method.
- The `Dog` class also has its own `bark()` method, which is specific to the dog behavior.

Accessing Base Class Members in Derived Class:

You can access members of the base class in the derived class, but there are some restrictions depending on whether the members are `public`, `protected`, or `private`.

- **Public members**: Accessible from anywhere, including derived classes.
- **Protected members**: Accessible within the class and its derived classes but not from outside.
- **Private members**: Not accessible in derived classes.

Example with Access Specifiers:

cpp

```cpp
#include <iostream>
using namespace std;

class Shape {
protected:
    int width, height;

public:
    Shape(int w, int h) : width(w), height(h) {}

    void display() {
        cout << "Width: " << width << ", Height: " <<
height << endl;
    }
};

class Rectangle : public Shape {
public:
    Rectangle(int w, int h) : Shape(w, h) {}
```

```
    int area() {
        return width * height;   // Accessing
protected member of the base class
    }
};

int main() {
    Rectangle rect(5, 10);
    rect.display();
    cout << "Area: " << rect.area() << endl;

    return 0;
}
```

In this example:

- The `Rectangle` class inherits from `Shape` and uses the constructor of the base class to initialize `width` and `height`.
- The `Rectangle` class has a method `area()` that calculates the area of the rectangle.

Polymorphism: Function Overriding and Overloading

Polymorphism is another core OOP concept that allows objects of different classes to be treated as objects of a common base class. It allows the same function to behave differently depending on the type of object it is called on.

Types of Polymorphism:

1. **Compile-time Polymorphism (Static Polymorphism):** Achieved through **function overloading** and **operator overloading**.
2. **Run-time Polymorphism (Dynamic Polymorphism):** Achieved through **function overriding** using **virtual functions**.

Function Overloading (Compile-Time Polymorphism)

Function overloading is the ability to define multiple functions with the same name but different parameters. C++ uses the number and types of arguments to differentiate between overloaded functions.

Example:

cpp

```cpp
#include <iostream>
using namespace std;

class Print {
public:
    // Function to print an integer
    void show(int i) {
        cout << "Integer: " << i << endl;
    }

    // Function to print a double
    void show(double d) {
        cout << "Double: " << d << endl;
    }
};

int main() {
    Print p;
    p.show(5);          // Calls show(int)
    p.show(5.5);        // Calls show(double)

    return 0;
}
```

Explanation:

- The show() function is overloaded to print either an integer or a double, depending on the argument type.

Function Overriding (Run-Time Polymorphism)

Function overriding allows a derived class to provide its specific implementation of a function that is already defined in the base class. This is possible if the function in the base class is marked as `virtual`.

Example:
cpp

```cpp
#include <iostream>
using namespace std;

class Animal {
public:
    virtual void sound() {   // Virtual function
        cout << "Some sound..." << endl;
    }
};

class Dog : public Animal {
public:
    void sound() override {   // Overriding the base
class function
        cout << "Bark!" << endl;
    }
};

class Cat : public Animal {
public:
    void sound() override {   // Overriding the base
class function
        cout << "Meow!" << endl;
    }
};

int main() {
    Animal* animal;

    Dog dog;
    Cat cat;
```

```
    // Polymorphism: base class pointer can point to
derived class objects
    animal = &dog;
    animal->sound();   // Calls Dog's sound()

    animal = &cat;
    animal->sound();   // Calls Cat's sound()

    return 0;
}
```

Explanation:

- **Virtual Function**: The sound() function in the Animal class is marked as virtual. This tells C++ to dynamically bind the function call at runtime.
- **Function Overriding**: The Dog and Cat classes override the sound() function to provide their own behavior.
- **Run-time Polymorphism**: The animal pointer can point to either a Dog or a Cat object, and the correct version of sound() is called at runtime.

Abstract Classes and Interfaces

An **abstract class** is a class that cannot be instantiated directly. It is meant to be inherited by other classes. Abstract classes are used to define a common interface and provide some base functionality, while leaving other details to be implemented by derived classes.

Abstract Classes:

An abstract class is declared by including at least one **pure virtual function**. A pure virtual function is a function declared in the base class that has no implementation in the base class itself.

Syntax for Pure Virtual Functions:

cpp

```cpp
class Base {
public:
    virtual void functionName() = 0;   // Pure virtual
function
};
```

- = 0 indicates that the function is pure virtual and must be overridden in the derived class.

Example of Abstract Class:

cpp

```cpp
#include <iostream>
using namespace std;

class Shape {
public:
    virtual void draw() = 0;   // Pure virtual
function
};

class Circle : public Shape {
public:
    void draw() override {
        cout << "Drawing a Circle" << endl;
    }
};

class Rectangle : public Shape {
public:
    void draw() override {
        cout << "Drawing a Rectangle" << endl;
    }
};

int main() {
    Shape* shape;

    Circle circle;
```

```
    Rectangle rectangle;

    shape = &circle;
    shape->draw();  // Calls Circle's draw()

    shape = &rectangle;
    shape->draw();  // Calls Rectangle's draw()

    return 0;
}
```

Explanation:

- The Shape class is an abstract class with a pure virtual
  function draw().
- The Circle and Rectangle classes derive from Shape and
  implement the draw() function.
- **Interfaces**: In C++, interfaces are typically created using
  abstract classes. An interface is simply an abstract class that
  contains only pure virtual functions and no data members.

Project: Building an Inventory Management System with Inheritance

Now that we have covered inheritance, polymorphism, and
abstraction, let's apply these concepts by building an **Inventory
Management System**. This system will allow us to manage different
types of products, each with different properties and behaviors.

Project Objective:

- We will create an abstract class Product that will serve as
  the base class.
- We will create two derived classes: ElectronicProduct
  and ClothingProduct.

- Each product type will have different attributes and methods, but both will share a common interface for displaying their details.

Code Implementation:
cpp

```cpp
#include <iostream>
#include <string>
using namespace std;

// Abstract class
class Product {
public:
    virtual void displayDetails() = 0;  // Pure
virtual function
    virtual double calculatePrice() = 0;  //
Calculate price based on product type
};

// Derived class: ElectronicProduct
class ElectronicProduct : public Product {
private:
    string name;
    double price;
    int warranty;

public:
    ElectronicProduct(string n, double p, int w) :
name(n), price(p), warranty(w) {}

    void displayDetails() override {
        cout << "Electronic Product: " << name <<
endl;
        cout << "Price: $" << price << endl;
        cout << "Warranty: " << warranty << " years"
<< endl;
    }

    double calculatePrice() override {
        return price + (price * 0.1);  // Adding 10%
tax for electronics
    }
```

```cpp
};

// Derived class: ClothingProduct
class ClothingProduct : public Product {
private:
    string name;
    double price;
    string size;

public:
    ClothingProduct(string n, double p, string s) :
name(n), price(p), size(s) {}

    void displayDetails() override {
        cout << "Clothing Product: " << name << endl;
        cout << "Price: $" << price << endl;
        cout << "Size: " << size << endl;
    }

    double calculatePrice() override {
        return price;  // No extra charge for
clothing
    }
};

int main() {
    Product* product1 = new
ElectronicProduct("Laptop", 999.99, 2);
    Product* product2 = new ClothingProduct("T-
shirt", 19.99, "M");

    product1->displayDetails();
    cout << "Price after tax: $" << product1-
>calculatePrice() << endl;

    product2->displayDetails();
    cout << "Price: $" << product2->calculatePrice()
<< endl;

    delete product1;
    delete product2;

    return 0;
}
```

<u>Explanation of the Code:</u>

- **Product Class**: The `Product` class is an abstract base class with pure virtual functions `displayDetails()` and `calculatePrice()`. This ensures that all derived classes implement these methods.
- **ElectronicProduct Class**: This class represents electronic items. It inherits from `Product` and implements the `displayDetails()` and `calculatePrice()` methods.
- **ClothingProduct Class**: This class represents clothing items. It also inherits from `Product` and implements the required methods.
- **Polymorphism**: In `main()`, we create objects of type `ElectronicProduct` and `ClothingProduct`, but treat them as `Product` pointers. This demonstrates the flexibility of polymorphism, where the correct method is called based on the actual object type at runtime.

Conclusion

In this chapter, we explored more advanced OOP principles that are essential for creating flexible and scalable systems. We covered:

- **Inheritance**: The ability to create new classes based on existing ones, allowing for code reuse and extension.
- **Polymorphism**: The ability to treat different objects as instances of a common base class, enabling dynamic behavior through function overriding and overloading.
- **Abstraction**: The concept of hiding complex implementation details and exposing only the essential features through abstract classes and interfaces.

We applied these principles in a practical **Inventory Management System**, demonstrating how inheritance and polymorphism can be used to manage different product types efficiently.

Chapter 10: C++ Standard Library and STL Containers

Objective:
In this chapter, we will explore the **C++ Standard Library (STL)** and some of the most commonly used **containers** and **algorithms** that it offers. The STL is a powerful collection of generic classes and functions that provide commonly used data structures, like **vectors**, **maps**, and **sets**, as well as algorithms to manipulate these structures. By understanding the STL, you can leverage its efficient and flexible tools to simplify your C++ programs. We will also cover how **iterators** work and how you can apply them with STL containers. Finally, we will apply these concepts in a **To-Do List Manager project** that uses STL containers to store and manage tasks.

What is the C++ Standard Library (STL)?

The **C++ Standard Library (STL)** is a collection of pre-written classes and functions that provide functionality commonly used in C++ programs. The STL includes tools for:

- **Data structures** (containers like vectors, lists, maps, sets).
- **Algorithms** (searching, sorting, and other operations on data).
- **Iterators** (objects used to traverse through containers).
- **Utilities** (like pairs, functions, and more).

By using the STL, you can avoid reinventing the wheel by utilizing these robust, efficient tools for data management and operations.

The STL is built on **template programming,** which means the classes and functions are designed to work with any data type. This makes the STL very flexible and reusable in different contexts.

Key Components of the STL:

1. **Containers**: Store data in different structures (e.g., vectors, maps).
2. **Algorithms**: Perform operations on data stored in containers (e.g., sorting, searching).
3. **Iterators**: Provide a way to traverse the elements of containers.
4. **Function Objects**: Allow custom behavior to be passed to algorithms.

Vectors: Dynamic Arrays

A **vector** is one of the most commonly used containers in C++. It is a dynamic array that can grow or shrink in size as elements are added or removed. Unlike traditional arrays, vectors can automatically adjust their size without needing to be resized manually.

Declaring and Using Vectors

To use vectors in C++, you need to include the `<vector>` header. Vectors can store elements of any data type and automatically manage memory for you.

Basic Syntax for Vectors:

cpp

```
#include <vector>
using namespace std;

vector<int> v;   // Declares a vector of integers
```

Example of Vector Operations:
cpp

```cpp
#include <iostream>
#include <vector>
using namespace std;

int main() {
    vector<int> nums;   // Create an empty vector of
integers

    // Add elements to the vector
    nums.push_back(10);   // Add 10 at the end of the
vector
    nums.push_back(20);   // Add 20
    nums.push_back(30);   // Add 30

    // Display elements in the vector
    for (int i = 0; i < nums.size(); i++) {
        cout << nums[i] << " ";
    }

    cout << endl;

    // Remove the last element
    nums.pop_back();   // Removes 30

    // Display elements after removal
    for (int i = 0; i < nums.size(); i++) {
        cout << nums[i] << " ";
    }

    return 0;
}
```

Explanation:

- `push_back()` adds elements to the end of the vector.
- `pop_back()` removes the last element of the vector.
- `size()` returns the number of elements in the vector.

Output:

```
10 20 30
10 20
```

Vectors automatically handle memory management, resizing when necessary, which makes them an excellent choice for dynamic arrays.

Benefits of Using Vectors:

- **Dynamic resizing**: The size of the vector can increase or decrease as needed.
- **Efficient element access**: Elements are stored in contiguous memory, so you can access them quickly using indices.

Maps: Key-Value Pairs

A **map** is a container that stores data as **key-value pairs**. Each key is unique, and it maps to a corresponding value. Maps are useful when you need to associate values with unique identifiers (such as storing a list of employees with their unique IDs).

Declaring and Using Maps

To use maps in C++, include the `<map>` header.

cpp

```
#include <map>
using namespace std;

map<int, string> employees;  // A map that maps
integer IDs to employee names
```

Example of Map Operations:
cpp

```cpp
#include <iostream>
#include <map>
using namespace std;

int main() {
    map<int, string> employees;

    // Add key-value pairs to the map
    employees[101] = "John";
    employees[102] = "Alice";
    employees[103] = "Bob";

    // Accessing elements using keys
    cout << "Employee 101: " << employees[101] <<
endl;

    // Iterating through the map
    for (auto it = employees.begin(); it !=
employees.end(); ++it) {
        cout << "ID: " << it->first << ", Name: " <<
it->second << endl;
    }

    // Checking if a key exists
    if (employees.find(102) != employees.end()) {
        cout << "Employee 102 exists." << endl;
    }

    return 0;
}
```

Explanation:

- We create a `map<int, string>` to store employee IDs (as keys) and their names (as values).
- `employees[101]` accesses the value associated with the key `101`.
- We use an iterator to loop through the map and print all key-value pairs.
- `find()` checks if a key exists in the map.

Output:

yaml

```
Employee 101: John
ID: 101, Name: John
ID: 102, Name: Alice
ID: 103, Name: Bob
Employee 102 exists.
```

Benefits of Using Maps:

- **Fast lookups**: Maps use a balanced tree structure, which allows for fast lookups and insertions.
- **Key-value association**: They are ideal when you need to associate a key with a value.

Sets: Unique Values

A **set** is a container that stores unique elements, and it automatically sorts them. Sets are useful when you need to store a collection of unique items and you do not care about the order in which they are stored.

Declaring and Using Sets

To use sets in C++, include the `<set>` header.

cpp

```
#include <set>
using namespace std;

set<int> numbers;  // A set of integers
```

Example of Set Operations:

cpp

```cpp
#include <iostream>
#include <set>
using namespace std;

int main() {
    set<int> numbers;

    // Add elements to the set
    numbers.insert(10);
    numbers.insert(20);
    numbers.insert(30);
    numbers.insert(10);   // Duplicates are ignored

    // Display elements in the set
    for (int num : numbers) {
        cout << num << " ";
    }

    cout << endl;

    // Check if an element exists
    if (numbers.find(20) != numbers.end()) {
        cout << "20 is in the set." << endl;
    }

    return 0;
}
```

Explanation:

- `insert()` adds elements to the set. If an element already exists, it will not be added again (sets store only unique values).
- `find()` is used to check if an element exists in the set.

Output:

csharp

```
10 20 30
20 is in the set.
```

Benefits of Using Sets:

- **Unique elements**: Sets automatically handle uniqueness, so duplicates are not allowed.
- **Sorted order**: Elements are stored in sorted order by default.
- **Efficient searching**: Searching for an element in a set is fast due to its underlying tree structure.

Iterators and Algorithms

Iterators are used to traverse through the elements of containers (like vectors, maps, and sets). They work similarly to pointers, allowing you to access and modify elements in a container.

Using Iterators

To use iterators in C++, you can define an iterator based on the container type.

cpp

```
vector<int> nums = {1, 2, 3, 4, 5};
vector<int>::iterator it = nums.begin();
```

Example of Using Iterators:

cpp

```
#include <iostream>
#include <vector>
using namespace std;

int main() {
    vector<int> nums = {1, 2, 3, 4, 5};

    // Using an iterator to traverse the vector
    vector<int>::iterator it;
    for (it = nums.begin(); it != nums.end(); ++it) {
        cout << *it << " ";
```

```
    }
    cout << endl;
    return 0;
}
```

Explanation:

- The iterator `it` is used to traverse the vector `nums`. We use `*it` to dereference the iterator and access the value of the current element.

Common STL Algorithms:

The STL also provides a range of **algorithms** that can be used with containers. Some of the most commonly used algorithms include:

- `sort()`: Sorts elements in a container.
- `find()`: Searches for a specific element.
- `reverse()`: Reverses the order of elements in a container.

Example of Using Algorithms:

cpp

```cpp
#include <iostream>
#include <vector>
#include <algorithm>   // For sort
using namespace std;

int main() {
    vector<int> nums = {5, 3, 8, 1, 2};

    // Sort the vector
    sort(nums.begin(), nums.end());

    // Display sorted vector
    for (int num : nums) {
        cout << num << " ";
    }
```

```
    cout << endl;

    return 0;
}
```

Explanation:

- The `sort()` function is used to sort the elements of the vector in ascending order.
- The algorithm operates on iterators, which are passed to the `begin()` and `end()` methods of the container.

Project: Build a To-Do List Manager Using STL Containers

Now that we understand vectors, maps, sets, iterators, and algorithms, let's apply these concepts by building a **To-Do List Manager**. This program will allow users to add tasks, remove tasks, and display a list of tasks using STL containers.

Project Objective:

- Use a `vector` to store tasks.
- Allow the user to add, remove, and list tasks.
- Use a `map` to store tasks with a unique identifier (task ID).

Code Implementation:
cpp

```cpp
#include <iostream>
#include <vector>
#include <map>
#include <string>
using namespace std;

class ToDoList {
private:
```

```cpp
    map<int, string> tasks;
    int taskCounter;

public:
    ToDoList() {
        taskCounter = 1;  // Start task IDs from 1
    }

    // Add a task
    void addTask(string task) {
        tasks[taskCounter] = task;
        cout << "Task added: " << task << endl;
        taskCounter++;
    }

    // Remove a task by ID
    void removeTask(int id) {
        if (tasks.find(id) != tasks.end()) {
            tasks.erase(id);
            cout << "Task removed." << endl;
        } else {
            cout << "Task ID not found." << endl;
        }
    }

    // Display all tasks
    void displayTasks() {
        if (tasks.empty()) {
            cout << "No tasks to display." << endl;
            return;
        }
        cout << "To-Do List:" << endl;
        for (auto& task : tasks) {
            cout << "ID: " << task.first << " - " <<
task.second << endl;
        }
    }
};

int main() {
    ToDoList todo;

    // Adding tasks
    todo.addTask("Buy groceries");
```

```cpp
    todo.addTask("Complete C++ project");

    // Displaying tasks
    todo.displayTasks();

    // Removing a task
    todo.removeTask(1);

    // Displaying tasks again
    todo.displayTasks();

    return 0;
}
```

Explanation:

- We use a `map` to store tasks with a unique ID.
- The `addTask()` method adds a new task with a unique ID.
- The `removeTask()` method removes a task by its ID.
- The `displayTasks()` method prints all tasks in the list.

Sample Output:

```vbnet
Task added: Buy groceries
Task added: Complete C++ project
To-Do List:
ID: 1 - Buy groceries
ID: 2 - Complete C++ project
Task removed.
To-Do List:
ID: 2 - Complete C++ project
```

Conclusion

In this chapter, we explored the powerful tools provided by the **C++ Standard Library (STL)**. We covered:

- **Vectors**: Dynamic arrays that automatically resize.

- **Maps**: Containers that store key-value pairs.
- **Sets**: Containers that store unique values in sorted order.
- **Iterators and Algorithms**: How to traverse containers and apply common algorithms.

We also applied these concepts by building a **To-Do List Manager**, which demonstrated how to use STL containers to manage tasks efficiently

Chapter 11: File Input and Output (I/O)

Objective:

In this chapter, we will explore how to work with files in C++. File input and output (I/O) is an essential part of many applications, allowing them to read data from files and store results in files. We will cover the basics of **reading from files, writing to files**, and handling **errors** that can occur during file operations. Additionally, we will apply these concepts by creating a **Contact Book** program that stores and loads contact information from a file, demonstrating how file operations can be used to persist data.

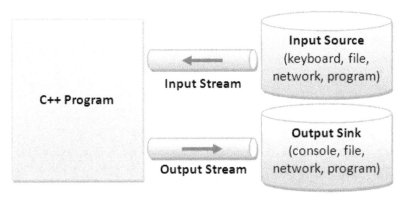

Internal Data Formats:
- Text: char, wchar_t
- int, float, double, etc.

External Data Formats:
- Text in various encodings (US-ASCII, ISO-8859-1, UCS-2, UTF-8, UTF-16, UTF-16BE, UTF16-LE, etc.)
- Binary (raw bytes)

What is File I/O in C++?

File I/O allows your program to interact with files, enabling you to read from files (input) or write data to files (output). This is crucial for applications that need to persist data, such as saving user preferences, storing logs, or managing databases.

C++ provides a set of functions and classes in the **fstream** library to perform file operations. The two main classes used for file handling are:

- **ifstream**: Used for reading from files (input file stream).
- **ofstream**: Used for writing to files (output file stream).
- **fstream**: Can be used for both reading from and writing to files.

The process of working with files involves the following steps:

1. **Opening a file**: You must open a file before you can read from or write to it.
2. **Reading or writing data**: Once the file is open, you can read from it or write data to it.
3. **Closing the file**: It's important to close the file after you are done to ensure all data is saved and resources are freed.

Reading from Files

To read from a file in C++, you use the `ifstream` class. The basic syntax is as follows:

cpp

```
#include <fstream>
#include <iostream>
#include <string>
using namespace std;
```

```
int main() {
    ifstream inputFile("filename.txt");  // Open file
for reading

    if (!inputFile) {  // Check if the file opened
successfully
        cerr << "File not found!" << endl;
        return 1;
    }

    string line;
    while (getline(inputFile, line)) {  // Read the
file line by line
        cout << line << endl;  // Output the line to
the console
    }

    inputFile.close();  // Close the file
    return 0;
}
```

Explanation:

- `ifstream inputFile("filename.txt");`: This opens the file "`filename.txt`" for reading.
- `getline(inputFile, line)`: This reads a line of text from the file into the `line` variable. The loop continues until the end of the file is reached.
- `inputFile.close();`: Always close the file when you're done reading.

If the file cannot be opened (e.g., if it doesn't exist), the program will print an error message and exit.

File Opening Modes

When working with files, you can specify how the file should be opened. Some common modes are:

- **ios::in**: Open the file for reading.
- **ios::out**: Open the file for writing (creates the file if it doesn't exist).
- **ios::app**: Append to the file (writes at the end of the file).
- **ios::binary**: Open the file in binary mode (useful for non-text files).

Writing to Files

To write to a file, you use the ofstream class. The basic syntax for writing to a file is:

cpp

```cpp
#include <fstream>
#include <iostream>
using namespace std;

int main() {
    ofstream outputFile("output.txt");   // Open file for writing

    if (!outputFile) {   // Check if the file opened successfully
        cerr << "File could not be opened!" << endl;
        return 1;
    }

    outputFile << "Hello, World!" << endl;   // Write to the file
    outputFile << "This is a test message." << endl;

    outputFile.close();   // Close the file
    return 0;
}
```

Explanation:

- `ofstream outputFile("output.txt");`: This opens the file `"output.txt"` for writing. If the file doesn't exist, it is created automatically.
- `outputFile << "Hello, World!" << endl;`: This writes the string `"Hello, World!"` to the file followed by a newline character.
- `outputFile.close();`: Always close the file after writing to it.

Appending to Files

If you want to add data to an existing file without overwriting it, use the `ios::app` flag:

cpp

```
ofstream outputFile("output.txt", ios::app);
```

This will open the file in append mode, and new data will be written at the end of the file.

Error Handling in File I/O

Error handling is crucial when working with files. There are several ways errors can occur, such as:

- The file may not exist.
- The program may not have permission to open the file.
- There may be an issue reading or writing to the file.

C++ provides several mechanisms to check for errors during file operations:

1. `if (!inputFile)`: Checks if the file was successfully opened for reading.

2. **if (!outputFile)**: Checks if the file was successfully opened for writing.
3. **fail()**: Returns true if the last file operation failed (e.g., reading from a file).
4. **eof()**: Returns true when the end of the file has been reached.

Example of Error Handling:

cpp

```cpp
#include <fstream>
#include <iostream>
using namespace std;

int main() {
    ifstream inputFile("nonexistentfile.txt");

    if (!inputFile) {
        cerr << "Error: Could not open the file!" <<
endl;
        return 1;
    }

    string content;
    getline(inputFile, content);

    if (inputFile.fail()) {
        cerr << "Error reading from file!" << endl;
    }

    inputFile.close();
    return 0;
}
```

Explanation:

- **if (!inputFile)**: This checks if the file could not be opened. If the file is missing or there's an issue with file permissions, the program prints an error message and exits.
- **fail()**: This checks if there was an error during reading.

Project: Create a Contact Book that Saves and Loads Data from Files

Let's apply what we've learned about file handling by building a **Contact Book** program. The program will allow users to add, view, and delete contacts, and it will save the contacts to a file so that the data persists between program runs.

Project Objective:

- The contact book will store **name** and **phone number** for each contact.
- The program will provide functionality to **add, display**, and **delete** contacts.
- All contacts will be saved in a file, and when the program starts, it will load the contacts from the file.

Code Implementation:
cpp

```
#include <iostream>
#include <fstream>
#include <vector>
#include <string>
using namespace std;

// Contact structure
struct Contact {
    string name;
    string phone;

    Contact(string n, string p) : name(n), phone(p)
{}
};

// Function to save contacts to a file
void saveContacts(const vector<Contact>& contacts) {
```

```cpp
    ofstream outputFile("contacts.txt", ios::trunc);
// Open file in truncate mode

    if (!outputFile) {
        cerr << "Error opening file for writing!" <<
endl;
        return;
    }

    for (const Contact& contact : contacts) {
        outputFile << contact.name << "," <<
contact.phone << endl;
    }

    outputFile.close();
}

// Function to load contacts from a file
void loadContacts(vector<Contact>& contacts) {
    ifstream inputFile("contacts.txt");

    if (!inputFile) {
        cerr << "Error opening file for reading!" <<
endl;
        return;
    }

    string name, phone;
    while (getline(inputFile, name, ',') &&
getline(inputFile, phone)) {
        contacts.push_back(Contact(name, phone));
    }

    inputFile.close();
}

// Function to display contacts
void displayContacts(const vector<Contact>& contacts)
{
    if (contacts.empty()) {
        cout << "No contacts to display." << endl;
        return;
    }
```

```cpp
    cout << "Contacts:" << endl;
    for (const Contact& contact : contacts) {
        cout << "Name: " << contact.name << ", Phone:
" << contact.phone << endl;
    }
}

int main() {
    vector<Contact> contacts;

    // Load contacts from file
    loadContacts(contacts);

    int choice;
    string name, phone;

    do {
        cout << "Contact Book Menu:" << endl;
        cout << "1. Add Contact" << endl;
        cout << "2. Display Contacts" << endl;
        cout << "3. Exit" << endl;
        cout << "Enter choice: ";
        cin >> choice;
        cin.ignore();  // Ignore the newline left by
cin

        switch (choice) {
            case 1:
                cout << "Enter name: ";
                getline(cin, name);
                cout << "Enter phone number: ";
                getline(cin, phone);

                contacts.push_back(Contact(name,
phone));
                saveContacts(contacts);
                break;

            case 2:
                displayContacts(contacts);
                break;

            case 3:
                cout << "Exiting program." << endl;
```

```
                break;

            default:
                cout << "Invalid choice! Please try
again." << endl;
                break;
        }

    } while (choice != 3);

    return 0;
}
```

Explanation of the Code:

- **Contact Structure**: The `Contact` structure holds the `name` and `phone` of each contact.
- **saveContacts()**: This function saves the contacts to a file. Each contact is stored on a separate line, with the name and phone number separated by a comma.
- **loadContacts()**: This function loads the contacts from the file when the program starts. It reads each line from the file, splits it into `name` and `phone`, and creates a `Contact` object for each line.
- **displayContacts()**: This function displays all the contacts stored in the `contacts` vector.
- **Main Menu**: The user can choose to add a contact, display all contacts, or exit the program. Contacts are saved to the file whenever a new contact is added.

Sample Output:

```mathematica
Contact Book Menu:
1. Add Contact
2. Display Contacts
3. Exit
Enter choice: 1
Enter name: John Doe
Enter phone number: 555-1234
```

```
Contact Book Menu:
1. Add Contact
2. Display Contacts
3. Exit
Enter choice: 2
Contacts:
Name: John Doe, Phone: 555-1234
```

File Storage:

The contacts are saved to a file called `contacts.txt`. Each line in the file contains the name and phone number of a contact, separated by a comma.

File Content (`contacts.txt`):

```
nginx
```

```
John Doe,555-1234
Jane Smith,555-5678
```

Conclusion

In this chapter, we covered **file input and output (I/O)** in C++, which is essential for reading and writing data to files. We learned how to:

- **Read from files** using `ifstream` and handle errors when the file cannot be opened.
- **Write to files** using `ofstream` and append data to existing files.
- **Handle errors** that can occur during file operations using the `fail()` and `eof()` functions.
- We applied these concepts by building a **Contact Book** program that saves and loads contact data from a file, demonstrating how to work with file I/O in a real-world application.

In the next chapter, we will explore **exception handling**, which will help you handle errors in a more structured way, making your programs more robust. Stay tuned for more!

Chapter 12: Exception Handling

Objective:
In this chapter, we will dive into the concept of **exception handling** in C++. Exception handling is a powerful mechanism that allows you to manage errors and exceptional situations that may arise during the execution of your program. Instead of having the program crash or behave unpredictably when an error occurs, exception handling allows you to gracefully handle errors and take appropriate actions. We will cover the basics of **exceptions**, how to use the **try, catch, and throw** mechanism, and how to define **custom exception classes**. By the end of this chapter, you'll have the knowledge to write more robust and fault-tolerant code. To apply what we learn, we will create a **program that handles user input errors gracefully**.

What Are Exceptions?

In C++, an **exception** is an event that occurs during the execution of a program that disrupts the normal flow of control. Exceptions are often errors or unusual conditions that can be handled in a controlled manner.

An exception can arise from a variety of sources:

- Invalid user input.
- Division by zero.
- Out-of-range array access.
- File I/O errors.

Without exception handling, if an error occurs, the program will often crash or behave in unexpected ways. With exception handling, you can catch the error, handle it, and allow the program to continue or fail gracefully.

Why Use Exception Handling?

1. **Separation of Concerns**: Exception handling allows you to separate error-handling code from regular logic, making your code cleaner and easier to maintain.
2. **Graceful Error Recovery**: You can define specific actions for error recovery, such as asking the user to enter valid data again.
3. **Prevent Program Crashes**: Rather than letting an error bring down the whole program, exceptions allow you to deal with it and proceed with the program's flow.

Try, Catch, and Throw

In C++, the mechanism for handling exceptions is built around three keywords:

- `try`: Defines a block of code that may throw an exception.
- `throw`: Used to throw an exception when something goes wrong.
- `catch`: Catches the exception and defines how to handle it.

Basic Syntax:
cpp

```
try {
    // Code that may throw an exception
} catch (ExceptionType& e) {
    // Handle the exception
}
```

- **try Block**: This is the section of code that you suspect may cause an error. If an error occurs inside this block, an exception is thrown.
- **throw**: When an error is detected in the try block, you use throw to send the exception to the catch block.
- **catch Block**: This block catches the exception thrown by the try block. You can handle the error in this block by either logging it, fixing the issue, or notifying the user.

Example:
cpp

```cpp
#include <iostream>
using namespace std;

int main() {
    try {
        int num1, num2;
        cout << "Enter two numbers: ";
        cin >> num1 >> num2;

        if (num2 == 0) {
            throw "Division by zero error!";
        }

        cout << "Result: " << num1 / num2 << endl;
    } catch (const char* msg) {
        cout << "Error: " << msg << endl;
    }

    return 0;
}
```

Explanation:

- In the try block, we check if the second number is zero before performing division.
- If num2 is zero, a throw statement is executed to throw a string error message "Division by zero error!".

- The `catch` block catches the exception and prints the error message.

Output:

```vbnet
Enter two numbers: 10 0
Error: Division by zero error!
```

Throwing Exceptions

You can throw exceptions of any data type, but typically, you'll throw either built-in types (like `int`, `double`, or `const char*`) or custom exception objects.

Throwing an Exception:
cpp

```
throw exception_object;
```

- `exception_object` can be a primitive data type, a standard library exception, or an object of a custom exception class.

Example of Throwing an Exception:
cpp

```cpp
#include <iostream>
using namespace std;

void divide(int a, int b) {
    if (b == 0) {
        throw "Cannot divide by zero!";
    } else {
        cout << "Result: " << a / b << endl;
    }
}

int main() {
```

```
    try {
        divide(10, 0);   // This will throw an
exception
    } catch (const char* msg) {
        cout << "Error: " << msg << endl;
    }

    return 0;
}
```

Custom Exception Classes

C++ allows you to define **custom exception classes** to handle specific error types in a more organized way. Custom exceptions are particularly useful when you want to provide more detailed error information or handle different types of errors in different ways.

Defining a Custom Exception Class:

To define a custom exception class, inherit from the standard exception class provided by C++ and override the what() function, which returns a descriptive error message.

Syntax for Custom Exception Class:
cpp

```cpp
#include <exception>   // For standard exception class
#include <iostream>
#include <string>
using namespace std;

class MyException : public exception {
public:
    const char* what() const throw() {
        return "Custom exception occurred!";
    }
};
```

Example:

```cpp
#include <iostream>
#include <exception>  // For standard exception class
using namespace std;

class InsufficientBalanceException : public exception
{
public:
    const char* what() const throw() {
        return "Insufficient balance for this
transaction!";
    }
};

class BankAccount {
private:
    double balance;

public:
    BankAccount(double initialBalance) :
balance(initialBalance) {}

    void withdraw(double amount) {
        if (amount > balance) {
            throw InsufficientBalanceException();  //
Throw custom exception
        } else {
            balance -= amount;
            cout << "Withdrawal successful. New
balance: " << balance << endl;
        }
    }
};

int main() {
    BankAccount account(100);

    try {
        account.withdraw(150);  // This will throw
the custom exception
    } catch (InsufficientBalanceException& e) {
        cout << "Error: " << e.what() << endl;
```

```
    }

    return 0;
}
```

Explanation:

- The `InsufficientBalanceException` class inherits from the `exception` class and overrides the `what()` method to provide a custom error message.
- In the `BankAccount` class, the `withdraw()` method throws this custom exception when a withdrawal amount exceeds the available balance.
- In the `main()` function, we catch the custom exception and print its message.

Output:

```javascript
Error: Insufficient balance for this transaction!
```

Project: Build a Program That Handles User Input Errors Gracefully

Let's apply what we've learned by building a program that handles **user input errors** gracefully. We will create a simple program where the user is asked to enter a number, and the program will handle invalid input (e.g., non-numeric characters or division by zero).

Project Objective:

- The program will ask the user to enter two numbers.
- It will handle **non-numeric input** and **division by zero** errors using exceptions.
- It will keep asking for valid input until the user provides it.

Code Implementation:
cpp

```cpp
#include <iostream>
#include <stdexcept>
#include <limits>  // For numeric_limits
using namespace std;

class InvalidInputException : public exception {
public:
    const char* what() const throw() {
        return "Invalid input! Please enter a valid
number.";
    }
};

class DivisionByZeroException : public exception {
public:
    const char* what() const throw() {
        return "Error: Division by zero is not
allowed!";
    }
};

double getNumber() {
    double number;
    while (true) {
        cout << "Enter a number: ";
        cin >> number;

        if (cin.fail()) {  // Check for non-numeric
input
            cin.clear();  // Clear the error flag

cin.ignore(numeric_limits<streamsize>::max(), '\n');
// Ignore bad input
            throw InvalidInputException();
        }
        return number;
    }
}

double divide(double num1, double num2) {
    if (num2 == 0) {
```

```
            throw DivisionByZeroException();
    }
    return num1 / num2;
}

int main() {
    double num1, num2;

    try {
        num1 = getNumber();
        num2 = getNumber();
        double result = divide(num1, num2);
        cout << "Result: " << result << endl;
    } catch (const InvalidInputException& e) {
        cout << "Error: " << e.what() << endl;
    } catch (const DivisionByZeroException& e) {
        cout << "Error: " << e.what() << endl;
    }

    return 0;
}
```

Explanation of the Code:

- **InvalidInputException**: A custom exception class to handle non-numeric input.
- **DivisionByZeroException**: A custom exception class to handle division by zero errors.
- **getNumber()**: This function asks the user to input a number. If the input is invalid (non-numeric), it throws an InvalidInputException.
- **divide()**: This function divides two numbers. If the second number is zero, it throws a DivisionByZeroException.
- **main()**: In the main() function, we try to get two valid numbers from the user and perform the division. If any exception is thrown, it is caught and handled gracefully.

Sample Output:

```vbnet
Enter a number: 10
Enter a number: 0
Error: Error: Division by zero is not allowed!
```

Conclusion

In this chapter, we introduced **exception handling** in C++, which is essential for managing errors and ensuring your programs run smoothly. We covered:

- **What exceptions are**: Errors or exceptional events that disrupt the normal flow of the program.
- **Try, Catch, and Throw**: How to use these keywords to catch and handle exceptions.
- **Custom exception classes**: How to create your own exception types to handle specific errors.
- We applied these concepts by building a **program that handles user input errors gracefully**, demonstrating how to catch and handle exceptions for invalid input and division by zero.

Exception handling allows you to write more resilient, user-friendly programs

Chapter 13: Working with Libraries

Objective:
In this chapter, we will explore how to **extend the functionality of your C++ programs** by integrating **third-party libraries**. Libraries provide pre-written code that allows you to perform complex tasks without having to reinvent the wheel. By the end of this chapter, you will understand how to install and use libraries in C++, and you will gain hands-on experience with three popular libraries: **Boost, SFML (Simple and Fast Multimedia Library)**, and **OpenCV**. We will conclude the chapter by building a **basic game** using **SFML**, which will involve working with graphics and sound.

What Are Libraries?

In programming, a **library** is a collection of pre-written code that provides specific functionality. These functions, classes, and modules are designed to perform common tasks, which saves you from having to write everything from scratch. For example, if you need to work with **file systems, networking, math operations**, or **graphics**, there are libraries available that provide ready-made solutions.

In C++, libraries can be:

- **Standard Libraries**: The C++ Standard Library, which includes useful tools like containers (e.g., vectors, maps), algorithms, and input/output facilities.

- **Third-Party Libraries**: These are external libraries that you can add to your projects to extend functionality. Examples include Boost, SFML, OpenCV, and many others.

By integrating third-party libraries, you can focus on the unique aspects of your program without needing to write every feature from scratch. Using libraries is a common practice in software development to boost productivity, improve code quality, and enable advanced features.

Installing and Using Libraries in C++

Before you can use a third-party library in your C++ project, you need to **install** it. The installation process typically involves downloading the library and linking it to your project. Below are the general steps for installing and using libraries in C++.

1. Installing Libraries

Most third-party libraries come with installation instructions. Here's how to install libraries on different systems:

- **Windows**: You can download precompiled libraries or use package managers like **vcpkg** or **Conan**.
- **Linux**: On Linux, you can install libraries using the system's package manager (e.g., `apt` on Ubuntu, `yum` on CentOS), or by downloading and compiling the source code.
- **macOS**: macOS also supports package managers like **Homebrew** for easy installation of libraries.

For example, to install the **Boost** library using **vcpkg** (a popular C++ package manager), you can follow these steps:

1. Install **vcpkg** from its official GitHub repository.
2. Use `vcpkg` to install Boost:

```bash
./vcpkg install boost
```

Once Boost is installed, you can link it to your project.

2. Linking the Library to Your Project

After installing a library, you need to **link it** to your C++ project. This involves adding the library's header files and binary files to your project configuration.

For example, if you are using **Visual Studio**, you can add include paths and link the necessary `.lib` files to your project settings. In **g++ (GNU Compiler)**, you can specify the path to the library using the `-I` (for include directories) and `-L` (for library directories) flags when compiling.

For example:

```bash
g++ -o my_program my_program.cpp -I/path/to/boost/include -L/path/to/boost/lib -lboost_system
```

This tells the compiler where to find the Boost headers and the Boost library files.

Common Libraries in C++

Now that you know how to install and link libraries to your projects, let's dive into three popular and widely used C++ libraries: **Boost, SFML**, and **OpenCV**.

Boost

The **Boost** library is a collection of free, peer-reviewed C++ libraries that extend the functionality of the C++ Standard Library. Boost includes libraries for:

- **Containers and data structures**.
- **Algorithms** for manipulating data.
- **Multithreading** and concurrency.
- **Filesystem** handling.
- **Networking**.

One of the most useful features of Boost is that it contains libraries that are often considered part of the C++ Standard Library, such as **Boost.Asio** for networking and **Boost.Filesystem** for file operations.

Example of Boost Usage:
cpp

```cpp
#include <boost/algorithm/string.hpp>
#include <iostream>
using namespace std;

int main() {
    string text = "Hello, Boost Library!";

    boost::to_upper(text);   // Convert text to uppercase using Boost
    cout << text << endl;    // Output: HELLO, BOOST LIBRARY!

    return 0;
}
```

Explanation:

- `boost::to_upper()` is used to convert a string to uppercase. Boost provides many such utilities that simplify common tasks.

SFML (Simple and Fast Multimedia Library)

SFML is a multimedia library that provides simple and easy-to-use interfaces for handling graphics, sound, windowing, and input devices. SFML is commonly used for developing 2D games or applications with graphical user interfaces (GUIs). It's an excellent library for learning game development or creating interactive applications.

SFML allows you to:

- Create **windows** and handle **events**.
- Render **2D graphics** (shapes, textures, sprites).
- Play **sound and music**.
- Handle **keyboard**, **mouse**, and **joystick** input.

Example of SFML Usage:

To begin using SFML, you will need to install it (like the Boost library). After that, you can start working with graphics and sound.

cpp

```cpp
#include <SFML/Graphics.hpp>
#include <SFML/Audio.hpp>

int main() {
    // Create a window
    sf::RenderWindow window(sf::VideoMode(800, 600),
"SFML Game");

    // Load a texture
    sf::Texture texture;
    if (!texture.loadFromFile("sprite.png")) {
        return -1;  // Error loading texture
    }

    // Create a sprite
```

```
        sf::Sprite sprite(texture);

        // Load sound
        sf::SoundBuffer buffer;
        if (!buffer.loadFromFile("sound.wav")) {
            return -1;  // Error loading sound
        }
        sf::Sound sound;
        sound.setBuffer(buffer);

        // Main game loop
        while (window.isOpen()) {
            sf::Event event;
            while (window.pollEvent(event)) {
                if (event.type == sf::Event::Closed)
                    window.close();
            }

            // Clear the screen
            window.clear();

            // Draw the sprite
            window.draw(sprite);

            // Display the window
            window.display();

            // Play sound when spacebar is pressed
            if
(sf::Keyboard::isKeyPressed(sf::Keyboard::Space)) {
                sound.play();
            }
        }

        return 0;
}
```

Explanation:

- **sf::RenderWindow** creates a window for the game.
- **sf::Texture** loads an image file to be used as a sprite.
- **sf::Sound** plays a sound when triggered by the user (in this case, the spacebar).

SFML is ideal for 2D games and simple multimedia applications, providing a range of functionality in an easy-to-use package.

OpenCV (Open Source Computer Vision Library)

OpenCV is one of the most popular and comprehensive libraries for computer vision. It provides tools for:

- **Image processing** (e.g., filters, transformations).
- **Object detection and recognition**.
- **Facial recognition**.
- **Machine learning** related to vision tasks.

OpenCV can be used for real-time video processing, object tracking, and various applications in robotics, security, and automation.

Example of OpenCV Usage:
cpp

```cpp
#include <opencv2/opencv.hpp>
#include <iostream>

int main() {
    // Load an image
    cv::Mat image = cv::imread("image.jpg");

    // Check if the image is loaded properly
    if (image.empty()) {
        std::cerr << "Could not open or find the image!" << std::endl;
        return -1;
    }

    // Convert the image to grayscale
    cv::Mat grayImage;
    cv::cvtColor(image, grayImage, cv::COLOR_BGR2GRAY);

    // Display the image
```

```
cv::imshow("Grayscale Image", grayImage);

// Wait for any key press to close the window
cv::waitKey(0);

return 0;
}
```

Explanation:

- `cv::imread()` loads an image from a file.
- `cv::cvtColor()` converts the image to grayscale.
- `cv::imshow()` displays the processed image in a window.

OpenCV provides an extensive set of tools for processing images and videos, making it an essential library for anyone working with computer vision.

Project: Creating a Basic Game Using SFML (Graphics and Sound)

In this section, we'll apply what we've learned about SFML by creating a simple game. This project will involve graphics, sound, and basic user interaction.

Project Objective:

- We will create a **Pong-style** game where two players control paddles to bounce a ball back and forth.
- The game will include **sound effects** for bouncing the ball.
- The game will use **SFML graphics** to display the paddles and ball.

Code Implementation:

cpp

```cpp
#include <SFML/Graphics.hpp>
#include <SFML/Audio.hpp>

int main() {
    // Create a window
    sf::RenderWindow window(sf::VideoMode(800, 600),
"Pong Game");

    // Create paddles
    sf::RectangleShape leftPaddle(sf::Vector2f(20,
100));
    leftPaddle.setPosition(50, 250);
    leftPaddle.setFillColor(sf::Color::Green);

    sf::RectangleShape rightPaddle(sf::Vector2f(20,
100));
    rightPaddle.setPosition(730, 250);
    rightPaddle.setFillColor(sf::Color::Red);

    // Create the ball
    sf::CircleShape ball(10);
    ball.setPosition(400, 300);
    ball.setFillColor(sf::Color::White);

    // Set ball speed
    sf::Vector2f ballSpeed(0.2f, 0.2f);

    // Load sound
    sf::SoundBuffer buffer;
    if (!buffer.loadFromFile("bounce.wav")) {
        std::cerr << "Error loading sound!" <<
std::endl;
        return -1;
    }
    sf::Sound bounceSound;
    bounceSound.setBuffer(buffer);

    // Main game loop
    while (window.isOpen()) {
        sf::Event event;
        while (window.pollEvent(event)) {
```

```
            if (event.type == sf::Event::Closed)
                window.close();
        }

        // Paddle movement
        if
(sf::Keyboard::isKeyPressed(sf::Keyboard::W) &&
leftPaddle.getPosition().y > 0)
            leftPaddle.move(0, -0.5f);
        if
(sf::Keyboard::isKeyPressed(sf::Keyboard::S) &&
leftPaddle.getPosition().y < 500)
            leftPaddle.move(0, 0.5f);
        if
(sf::Keyboard::isKeyPressed(sf::Keyboard::Up) &&
rightPaddle.getPosition().y > 0)
            rightPaddle.move(0, -0.5f);
        if
(sf::Keyboard::isKeyPressed(sf::Keyboard::Down) &&
rightPaddle.getPosition().y < 500)
            rightPaddle.move(0, 0.5f);

        // Ball movement
        ball.move(ballSpeed);

        // Ball collision with top and bottom
        if (ball.getPosition().y <= 0 ||
ball.getPosition().y >= 590) {
            ballSpeed.y = -ballSpeed.y;  // Reverse
vertical direction
            bounceSound.play();
        }

        // Ball collision with paddles
        if
(ball.getGlobalBounds().intersects(leftPaddle.getGlob
alBounds()) ||

ball.getGlobalBounds().intersects(rightPaddle.getGlob
alBounds())) {
            ballSpeed.x = -ballSpeed.x;  // Reverse
horizontal direction
            bounceSound.play();
        }
```

```
    // Clear the window
    window.clear();

    // Draw everything
    window.draw(leftPaddle);
    window.draw(rightPaddle);
    window.draw(ball);

    // Display the window
    window.display();
  }

  return 0;
}
```

Explanation:

- **SFML Window**: We create a window of size `800x600` for the game.
- **Paddles**: `sf::RectangleShape` objects represent the left and right paddles.
- **Ball**: A `sf::CircleShape` represents the ball.
- **Movement**: The ball moves continuously, bouncing off the top and bottom walls and reversing direction when it hits a paddle.
- **Sound**: We use `sf::Sound` to play a sound every time the ball hits the paddle or a wall.

Running the Game:

The game runs in a loop, updating the ball and paddle positions and checking for collisions. The sound effect plays whenever the ball bounces off the paddle or wall.

Conclusion

In this chapter, we learned how to **extend the functionality of our C++ programs** by integrating third-party libraries. We covered:

- **Installing and using libraries**: How to install and link libraries to your C++ projects.
- **Common libraries**: We explored **Boost, SFML**, and **OpenCV**, which are widely used in various domains like general-purpose programming, game development, and computer vision.
- We built a **Pong-style game using SFML**, demonstrating how to use libraries for graphics, sound, and user input.

With the knowledge gained from this chapter, you can now start integrating powerful third-party libraries into your C++ projects to enhance their capabilities and build more complex systems.

Chapter 14: Introduction to C++ with Microservices

Objective:
In this chapter, we will introduce the concept of **microservices** and demonstrate how **C++** can be used to design scalable and efficient applications that follow the **microservices architecture**. You'll learn about the fundamental principles behind microservices, how to design scalable systems, and how microservices communicate using **APIs** and **RESTful services**. By the end of this chapter, we will build a **simple microservice** using C++ to manage user data, giving you a hands-on understanding of implementing a real-world scalable system.

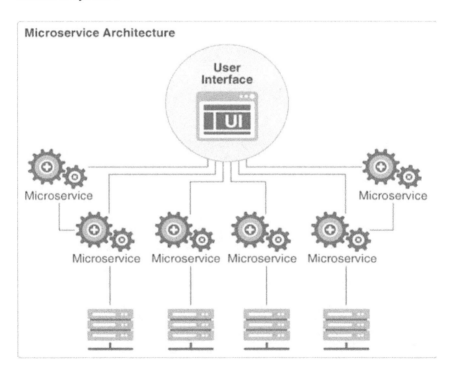

What Are Microservices?

The term **microservices** refers to an architectural style where an application is structured as a collection of loosely coupled services. Each service is focused on a single task or domain and is independently deployable, scalable, and maintainable. Microservices are typically small, modular services that communicate with each other through standard protocols, usually over the network.

Why Microservices?

Microservices provide several benefits:

1. **Modularity**: Each service is designed to perform one specific function. This modularity allows easier maintenance, updates, and scaling.
2. **Scalability**: Services can be scaled independently, meaning you can allocate resources more efficiently based on the needs of each service.
3. **Fault Isolation**: If one service fails, it doesn't necessarily bring down the whole application. This isolation improves the resilience of the system.
4. **Technology Agnostic**: Different microservices can be written in different programming languages or frameworks, based on the best fit for the task.
5. **Continuous Delivery and Deployment**: Microservices make it easier to deploy new features independently, enabling faster development cycles.

Designing Scalable Systems

When designing scalable systems with microservices, there are a few key principles and considerations to keep in mind:

1. Single Responsibility Principle (SRP)

Each microservice should be responsible for one specific domain or business capability. This means that every microservice should focus on a single task, making it easier to update, test, and maintain.

2. Independent Deployment and Scaling

Each microservice is deployed and scaled independently. This allows resources to be allocated based on the needs of each service rather than scaling the entire application. For example, a microservice that handles payments might need more resources during peak transaction hours, while a user service might require fewer resources.

3. Communication Between Microservices

Microservices need to communicate with each other, and this communication typically happens through **APIs** (Application Programming Interfaces). **REST** (Representational State Transfer) is one of the most commonly used protocols for microservice communication, where services interact over HTTP using standard methods such as `GET`, `POST`, `PUT`, and `DELETE`.

4. Data Management and Persistence

Each microservice should manage its own data. This ensures that the services are decoupled and that they don't rely on each other's databases. Services can communicate and share data through APIs, but each service manages its own storage independently.

5. Monitoring and Logging

Because microservices involve many independent services, it's crucial to have robust **monitoring** and **logging** systems to track the health of each service, ensure that everything is functioning correctly, and identify issues when they arise.

Connecting Microservices: APIs and REST

The most common way microservices communicate is through **APIs,** which allow them to expose specific functionality to other services or external clients. APIs define how different software components interact and provide an interface for communication.

In the context of microservices, the **REST architecture** is one of the most widely used approaches for building APIs. REST is based on HTTP and uses standard HTTP methods (GET, POST, PUT, DELETE) to perform CRUD (Create, Read, Update, Delete) operations on resources.

Key Concepts of RESTful APIs:

1. **Resources**: Each service exposes certain resources (e.g., user data, product information), which are accessed and manipulated using HTTP requests.
2. **Stateless Communication**: Every request to a REST API should contain all the information necessary for processing. The server should not store any session data between requests.
3. **Use of HTTP Methods**:
   - GET: Retrieve information (e.g., get a list of users).
   - POST: Create a new resource (e.g., add a new user).
   - PUT: Update an existing resource (e.g., update user details).
   - DELETE: Remove a resource (e.g., delete a user).

4. **HTTP Status Codes**: RESTful services use standard HTTP status codes to indicate the success or failure of a request (e.g., 200 for OK, 404 for Not Found, 500 for Server Error).

Example of a RESTful API:

Here's a simple conceptual example of how microservices communicate via RESTful APIs:

- **GET** `/users/`: Retrieves a list of users.
- **GET** `/users/{id}`: Retrieves details of a specific user by ID.
- **POST** `/users/`: Creates a new user.
- **PUT** `/users/{id}`: Updates an existing user by ID.
- **DELETE** `/users/{id}`: Deletes a user by ID.

Each of these endpoints would correspond to a specific function in the microservice, which handles requests, processes data, and returns the appropriate response.

Project: Designing a Simple Microservice to Manage User Data Using C++

Now that we understand the key concepts of microservices and REST, let's build a **simple microservice** using **C++** to manage user data. We will create a microservice that can perform basic CRUD operations: **Create**, **Read**, **Update**, and **Delete** user data.

For the purpose of this project, we will:

- Use **C++** for the backend logic.
- Use **REST** for communication between services.
- Store data in a simple **in-memory structure** (for demonstration purposes).

<u>Project Objective:</u>

- Implement a **User Management Service** that allows us to add, update, delete, and retrieve user information.
- Use **C++** to build the core functionality of the microservice.
- Use **RESTful APIs** to expose the service to other systems or microservices.
- For simplicity, we'll use a basic **JSON-like structure** to represent user data.

Step 1: Setting Up the REST Server

We'll use the **C++ REST SDK** (also known as **cpprestsdk**) to create a simple HTTP server for our microservice. The C++ REST SDK provides classes to handle HTTP requests, manage JSON data, and support RESTful APIs.

<u>Installing the C++ REST SDK:</u>

To use the C++ REST SDK, you need to install it. You can install it via **vcpkg** or **CMake**:

1. **Install using vcpkg:**

   ```bash
   vcpkg install cpprestsdk
   ```

2. **Using CMake:** Clone the repository from GitHub and follow the instructions in the README to build the library.

Step 2: Defining the User Data Model

Let's define a **User** class that will represent each user in our system. The user will have the following attributes:

- id (unique identifier)
- name (user's name)
- email (user's email)

Here is a basic C++ class that will represent our user data model:

cpp

```cpp
#include <string>
#include <iostream>
using namespace std;

class User {
public:
    int id;
    string name;
    string email;

    User(int id, const string& name, const string&
email) : id(id), name(name), email(email) {}

    void display() {
        cout << "ID: " << id << ", Name: " << name <<
", Email: " << email << endl;
    }
};
```

Step 3: Implementing the User Service

Now, let's implement the **UserService** class, which will manage the user data in memory. This service will be responsible for handling the CRUD operations.

cpp

```cpp
#include <vector>
#include <algorithm>
#include "User.h"

class UserService {
private:
    vector<User> users;

public:
    void addUser(const User& user) {
        users.push_back(user);
    }

    User* getUser(int id) {
        for (auto& user : users) {
            if (user.id == id) {
                return &user;
            }
        }
        return nullptr;
    }

    void updateUser(int id, const string& name, const
string& email) {
        User* user = getUser(id);
        if (user) {
            user->name = name;
            user->email = email;
        }
    }

    void deleteUser(int id) {
        auto it = std::remove_if(users.begin(),
users.end(), [id](const User& user) {
            return user.id == id;
        });
        users.erase(it, users.end());
    }

    void displayAllUsers() {
        for (const auto& user : users) {
            user.display();
        }
```

```
        }
};
```

Step 4: Setting Up REST Endpoints Using C++ REST SDK

We'll now set up a simple **HTTP server** using the **C++ REST SDK** to expose our user management service as a RESTful API.

Implementing the HTTP Server:
cpp

```cpp
#include <cpprest/http_listener.h>
#include <cpprest/json.h>
#include <cpprest/http_client.h>
#include <cpprest/json.h>
#include <string>
#include "UserService.h"

using namespace web;
using namespace web::http;
using namespace web::http::experimental::listener;
using namespace std;

class UserAPI {
private:
    http_listener listener;
    UserService userService;

public:
    UserAPI(const string& address) {
        listener = http_listener(address);
        listener.support(methods::GET,
bind(&UserAPI::handleGet, this,
std::placeholders::_1));
        listener.support(methods::POST,
bind(&UserAPI::handlePost, this,
std::placeholders::_1));
        listener.support(methods::PUT,
bind(&UserAPI::handlePut, this,
std::placeholders::_1));
```

```
        listener.support(methods::DEL,
bind(&UserAPI::handleDelete, this,
std::placeholders::_1));
    }

    void start() {
        listener
            .open()
            .then([this](){ cout << "Starting User
Service..." << endl; })
            .wait();
    }

    void handleGet(http_request request) {
        uri requested_uri = request.relative_uri();
        string path = requested_uri.path();
        int userId = stoi(path.substr(1));

        User* user = userService.getUser(userId);

        if (user) {
            json::value responseData;
            responseData[U("id")] =
json::value::number(user->id);
            responseData[U("name")] =
json::value::string(user->name);
            responseData[U("email")] =
json::value::string(user->email);

            request.reply(status_codes::OK,
responseData);
        } else {
            request.reply(status_codes::NotFound,
"User not found");
        }
    }

    void handlePost(http_request request) {

request.extract_json().then([this](json::value
requestData) {
            int id =
requestData[U("id")].as_integer();
```

```
            string name =
requestData[U("name")].as_string();
            string email =
requestData[U("email")].as_string();

            User user(id, name, email);
            userService.addUser(user);
            request.reply(status_codes::Created,
"User created successfully");
        }).wait();
    }

    void handlePut(http_request request) {

request.extract_json().then([this](json::value
requestData) {
            int id =
requestData[U("id")].as_integer();
            string name =
requestData[U("name")].as_string();
            string email =
requestData[U("email")].as_string();

            userService.updateUser(id, name, email);
            request.reply(status_codes::OK, "User
updated successfully");
        }).wait();
    }

    void handleDelete(http_request request) {
        uri requested_uri = request.relative_uri();
        int userId =
stoi(requested_uri.path().substr(1));

        userService.deleteUser(userId);
        request.reply(status_codes::OK, "User deleted
successfully");
    }
};
```

Step 5: Running the Microservice

Finally, we can start the **UserAPI** microservice and handle requests on different endpoints.

cpp

```cpp
int main() {
    UserAPI api("http://localhost:8080");
    api.start();

    string line;
    getline(cin, line);   // Keep the server running
until the user presses enter
    return 0;
}
```

Conclusion

In this chapter, we covered **microservices** and how to use **C++** to design scalable systems. We explored:

- **What microservices are** and the advantages of using microservices for scalability and flexibility.
- The principles of designing scalable systems, focusing on modularity, independent services, and effective communication using **APIs** and **REST**.
- We also built a **User Management Microservice** that provides basic CRUD operations to manage user data, demonstrating how to implement microservices in C++.

With the knowledge gained in this chapter, you can now begin building scalable applications using the microservices architecture in C++.

Chapter 15: Putting It All Together – A Capstone Project

Objective:
This chapter marks the culmination of everything we've learned in the previous chapters. We will combine all the key C++ concepts we've explored—such as object-oriented programming, file handling, microservices, error management, and more—into a **final project**. The goal of this chapter is to help you design, plan, and implement a complete system using the skills you've gained. Whether you're interested in building an **e-commerce system**, a **healthcare management system**, or a **small game**, this project will challenge you to apply C++ in a practical, real-world context.

Designing and Planning Your Final Project

Before jumping into the coding phase, it's crucial to **design** and **plan** your project thoroughly. Proper planning ensures that the project remains organized, and the final product is effective and scalable.

1. Define the Purpose and Scope

The first step is to define the **purpose** of your project and outline the **scope**. Here are some example ideas that combine various elements we've learned throughout the book:

- **E-commerce System**: A web-based system that allows users to browse products, add them to a shopping cart, and make purchases. This would involve user management, product data, shopping cart management, and payment processing.

- **Healthcare Management System**: A system that allows healthcare providers to manage patient records, appointments, and billing. This could include managing sensitive patient data and providing functionalities like searching for patient records or setting appointments.
- **Small Game**: A basic game that incorporates user input, graphics, sound, and possibly networking for multiplayer features. This would combine graphical programming with handling user inputs and game mechanics.

2. Break the Project into Smaller Modules

Once you've decided on the project idea, break it down into manageable modules or components. For example, if you're building an **e-commerce system**, some of the key modules might include:

- **User Authentication**: Handling user registration, login, and session management.
- **Product Management**: Displaying products, filtering them by categories, adding new products, and editing product details.
- **Shopping Cart and Checkout**: Adding products to a cart, updating quantities, and checking out (including handling payment).
- **Order Management**: Processing orders, updating stock, and tracking order status.

Each of these modules can be built and tested individually before integrating them into the final system.

3. Choose the Right Tools and Libraries

For your project, you might want to choose tools and libraries that will make your development process easier and more efficient. For example:

- **Boost**: A great library for working with data structures, algorithms, and multithreading.
- **SFML**: If you're building a game, SFML provides simple tools for graphics and sound.
- **OpenCV**: If your project involves image processing or computer vision, OpenCV can be incredibly useful.

In our capstone project, we'll be integrating **file handling**, **networking**, **user input**, and **error handling** to make the system robust.

Choosing a Project Idea

Now, let's discuss three potential project ideas in detail, so you can decide which one to build based on your interests and skill level.

1. E-commerce System (Intermediate to Advanced)

An **e-commerce system** requires integrating user input, file management, data validation, and possibly networking. Here's how you can approach this:

- **User Authentication**: Create a registration and login system where users can create accounts, log in, and view their purchase history. Use file handling to store user credentials securely.
- **Product Management**: Products should be stored in a structured format, like JSON or CSV files. You could also implement functionality for adding, editing, and deleting products.
- **Shopping Cart and Checkout**: Implement a shopping cart system where users can add, update, or remove items. For checkout, you could simulate payment processing by accepting user input for payment details.

- **Order Management**: Once an order is placed, store order details in a file. Optionally, you could send an email confirmation (using a simple SMTP client) or track order statuses (e.g., Pending, Shipped, Delivered).

2. Healthcare Management System (Advanced)

A **healthcare management system** is a more complex project that deals with sensitive information. Here's how you might break it down:

- **Patient Management**: Store and retrieve patient records, including medical history, contact information, and appointment details.
- **Appointment Scheduling**: Allow users to schedule, cancel, or view appointments. You could implement a calendar view for appointments.
- **Billing and Payment**: Generate invoices based on services provided and simulate payment processing.
- **Data Security**: Use file encryption or hashing for storing sensitive data like patient IDs or medical history.

3. Small Game (Intermediate)

If you enjoy creating interactive applications, a **small game** can be a fun and rewarding project. Here are some ideas for building a simple game:

- **Game Mechanics**: Implement game logic such as movement, collision detection, and scoring.
- **Graphics and Sound**: Use **SFML** to create graphics and add sound effects when certain actions occur in the game.
- **User Input**: Handle keyboard or mouse input for controlling game characters or elements.
- **Multiplayer (Optional)**: Use basic **networking** to connect multiple players in a game.

Step-by-Step Implementation: Using All C++ Concepts Learned

Now that we've chosen our project idea, let's break it down into smaller steps for implementation. We will focus on the **E-commerce System** idea for the capstone project, but the same principles can be applied to the other projects.

1. Setting Up the Project Structure

A clean and modular project structure is essential for easy maintenance and future scalability. Here's a suggested directory structure for the e-commerce system:

bash

```
/EcommerceSystem
    /src
        main.cpp
        UserManagement.cpp
        ProductManagement.cpp
        CartManagement.cpp
        OrderManagement.cpp
    /include
        UserManagement.h
        ProductManagement.h
        CartManagement.h
        OrderManagement.h
    /data
        users.txt
        products.csv
        orders.txt
    /assets
        /images
        /sounds
    /lib
        (Any external libraries like Boost, SFML,
etc.)
```

Each source file (`.cpp`) corresponds to a module of the system, and each header file (`.h`) contains the declarations for the functions and classes in that module. The `data` folder stores files containing persistent data like user information, product listings, and order records.

2. Designing the User Management Module

The **User Management Module** will handle user registration, login, and user profile management.

User Management Class:
cpp

```cpp
#include <iostream>
#include <fstream>
#include <string>
using namespace std;

class User {
public:
    string username;
    string password;

    User(string u, string p) : username(u),
password(p) {}
};

class UserManager {
private:
    string userFile = "data/users.txt";

public:
    void registerUser(string username, string
password) {
        ofstream file(userFile, ios::app);
        if (file.is_open()) {
            file << username << "," << password <<
endl;
            cout << "User registered successfully!"
<< endl;
```

```
        } else {
            cout << "Error registering user." <<
endl;
        }
        file.close();
    }

    bool loginUser(string username, string password)
{
        ifstream file(userFile);
        string storedUsername, storedPassword;

        while (getline(file, storedUsername, ',') &&
getline(file, storedPassword)) {
            if (storedUsername == username &&
storedPassword == password) {
                return true;   // Login successful
            }
        }

        return false;   // Login failed
    }
};
```

Explanation:

- The `UserManager` class handles both **user registration** and **login** functionality. When a new user is registered, their username and password are saved to a file (`users.txt`). When a user attempts to log in, their credentials are validated against the stored data.

3. Designing the Product Management Module

The **Product Management Module** will allow the system to manage product data.

Product Management Class:
cpp

```
#include <iostream>
```

```cpp
#include <fstream>
#include <vector>
#include <sstream>
using namespace std;

class Product {
public:
    int id;
    string name;
    double price;

    Product(int i, string n, double p) : id(i),
name(n), price(p) {}
};

class ProductManager {
private:
    string productFile = "data/products.csv";

public:
    void addProduct(int id, string name, double
price) {
        ofstream file(productFile, ios::app);
        if (file.is_open()) {
            file << id << "," << name << "," << price
<< endl;
            cout << "Product added successfully!" <<
endl;
        } else {
            cout << "Error adding product." << endl;
        }
        file.close();
    }

    vector<Product> getProducts() {
        ifstream file(productFile);
        vector<Product> products;
        string line;

        while (getline(file, line)) {
            stringstream ss(line);
            string idStr, name, priceStr;

            getline(ss, idStr, ',');
```

```
        getline(ss, name, ',');
        getline(ss, priceStr);

        int id = stoi(idStr);
        double price = stod(priceStr);
        products.push_back(Product(id, name,
price));
        }

    return products;
    }
};
```

Explanation:

- The `ProductManager` class handles **adding products** to a product list stored in `products.csv` and retrieving the list of products.
- Each product has an `id`, `name`, and `price`, and we use a CSV file format to store product data.

4. Integrating the System

Once we have implemented the user management and product management modules, we can integrate them into a main program that runs the e-commerce system.

cpp

```cpp
#include <iostream>
#include "UserManagement.cpp"
#include "ProductManagement.cpp"

int main() {
    UserManager userManager;
    ProductManager productManager;

    // Register a user
    userManager.registerUser("john_doe",
"password123");
```

```cpp
    // Login a user
    if (userManager.loginUser("john_doe",
"password123")) {
        cout << "Login successful!" << endl;
    } else {
        cout << "Login failed!" << endl;
    }

    // Add some products
    productManager.addProduct(1, "Laptop", 999.99);
    productManager.addProduct(2, "Smartphone",
599.99);

    // Display all products
    vector<Product> products =
productManager.getProducts();
    for (const Product& product : products) {
        cout << "ID: " << product.id << ", Name: " <<
product.name << ", Price: $" << product.price <<
endl;
    }

    return 0;
}
```

Step 4: Testing and Debugging

Once your project is implemented, thorough **testing** and **debugging** are necessary to ensure it works as expected. Here are a few tips for testing and debugging your application:

Unit Testing:

Test each module individually to ensure it functions correctly. For example, test the **UserManager** by registering and logging in users, and verify that the data is correctly stored and retrieved.

Integration Testing:

Test the integration of different modules. Ensure that when you register a user, they can then log in and access the products.

Error Handling:

Test edge cases, such as:

- Attempting to log in with incorrect credentials.
- Adding products with invalid data.
- Ensuring that the system handles invalid file operations gracefully.

Debugging:

Use a debugger to step through your code and track down any issues. You can also use logging to print out key values and catch errors early.

Conclusion

In this chapter, we combined everything learned throughout the book to build a complete **E-commerce System** using **C++**. We designed and planned the project, implemented key components like **user management** and **product management**, and tested the system to ensure its functionality. This capstone project allowed us to put **C++ concepts** into action and create a fully functional application.

With this knowledge, you can now tackle more complex projects and start integrating **microservices, multithreading, databases**, and **networking** into your C++ applications.

Conclusion: Moving Forward with C++

Objective:
As we reach the end of this book, it's time to reflect on the knowledge we've gained and look forward to the next steps in our journey with C++. We've explored a wide array of topics—from fundamental concepts like variables and loops to advanced subjects like microservices and custom exception handling. In this concluding chapter, we'll reflect on our journey through C++, provide direction on where to go next, and offer resources for continued learning. Finally, I'll leave you with some words of encouragement to help you stay motivated and keep building with C++.

Where to Go Next?

C++ is a powerful language that can be used for a wide range of applications, from system programming to game development, embedded systems, and more. Having completed this book, you now have a solid foundation in C++ programming, but there's so much more to explore. To take your C++ skills to the next level, you should start diving into more **advanced topics** that will challenge you and expand your knowledge.

Let's look at some of the next areas to explore in C++.

1. Multi-Threading in C++

One of the most exciting and useful features of C++ is the ability to write multi-threaded applications. Multi-threading allows you to execute multiple parts of a program simultaneously, improving performance and responsiveness—especially in applications like games, web servers, or data processing systems.

- **Why is Multi-Threading Important?**
  - In today's world of multi-core processors, multi-threading allows you to take full advantage of the hardware. Many tasks, such as web requests, background computation, or file I/O, can be executed in parallel, which drastically reduces runtime.
  - Multi-threading helps create **responsive systems**. For example, in game development, while one thread is responsible for rendering graphics, another can handle user input or networking without causing lag or freezes.
- **Key Concepts to Learn:**
  - **Threads**: Basic understanding of how to create and manage threads in C++.
  - **Mutexes and Locks**: How to ensure thread safety by using synchronization mechanisms like mutexes.
  - **Condition Variables**: Useful for communication between threads.
  - **Thread Pools**: Manage and reuse a set of threads for performing multiple tasks concurrently.

  C++ Standard Library Support: The C++ Standard Library has built-in support for threading starting from **C++11** with the `<thread>`, `<mutex>`, and `<condition_variable>` libraries. This makes it easier than ever to add multi-threading to your programs.

Resources for Learning Multi-Threading in C++:

- **Books:**
  - *C++ Concurrency in Action* by Anthony Williams
  - *Effective Modern C++* by Scott Meyers (contains multi-threading tips in modern C++)

- **Online Resources:**
  - C++ Multithreading Tutorial by cppreference.com
  - C++ Threading Guide by GeeksforGeeks

---

2. Design Patterns in C++

Design patterns are general reusable solutions to common problems that occur in software design. They provide best practices for solving complex design problems in an efficient and maintainable way. Understanding and implementing design patterns will make your code more robust, scalable, and easier to maintain.

- **Why Design Patterns Matter?**
  - They help **standardize** solutions to common problems, making your code more understandable to other developers.
  - By using well-established patterns, you can reduce the time spent solving design problems and improve the overall structure of your applications.
  - They provide **flexibility**. For example, in a microservices architecture, using patterns like **Factory** or **Observer** can help you manage service interactions effectively.
- **Key Design Patterns to Explore in C++:**
  - **Singleton**: Ensures that a class has only one instance and provides a global point of access to it.
  - **Factory**: Defines an interface for creating objects, but allows subclasses to alter the type of objects created.
  - **Observer**: Defines a one-to-many dependency between objects so that when one object changes state, all its dependents are notified and updated automatically.
  - **Strategy**: Allows a client to choose from a family of algorithms at runtime.

C++ Libraries for Design Patterns: You can also use libraries like **Boost** and **Qt** that provide implementations of various design patterns.

Resources for Learning Design Patterns:

- **Books:**
    - *Design Patterns: Elements of Reusable Object-Oriented Software* by Erich Gamma, Richard Helm, Ralph Johnson, and John Vlissides (known as the "Gang of Four")
    - *Head First Design Patterns* by Eric Freeman and Elisabeth Robson
    - *Design Patterns in Modern C++* by Dmitri Nesteruk
- **Online Resources:**
    - C++ Design Patterns - Refactoring.Guru
    - Design Patterns in C++ on GeeksforGeeks

---

3. C++ for Web Development

While C++ is traditionally known for its role in system-level programming and performance-critical applications, it can also be used for **web development**. Modern C++ frameworks provide tools for creating robust web applications, including both the front-end and back-end.

- **Why Learn Web Development in C++?**
    - **High performance**: C++ applications can handle very high loads and are suitable for performance-critical back-end services.
    - **Control over resources**: C++ gives you full control over memory management, which can be crucial for highly optimized systems.

- **Modern Frameworks**: Frameworks like **Crow** and **CppCMS** allow you to build web servers and applications in C++ with ease.
- **Key Concepts to Explore:**
  - **Web Servers**: Build a basic web server that can handle HTTP requests.
  - **REST APIs**: Learn how to create RESTful services in C++.
  - **Databases**: Connect your C++ application to a database using libraries like **MySQL Connector/C++**.

Resources for Learning C++ Web Development:

- **Books:**
  - *Web Development with C++ and the Wt Framework* by Jeroen van der Zijp
- **Online Resources:**
  - Crow Web Framework
  - CppCMS
  - Building REST APIs with C++

4. C++ in Game Development

C++ is one of the most widely used languages in **game development**, thanks to its performance, memory management capabilities, and control over hardware. Whether you're building 2D or 3D games, C++ remains a top choice for game developers.

- **Why C++ for Game Development?**
  - **Performance**: C++ provides the performance needed for real-time applications, which is crucial for smooth and responsive games.
  - **Memory Management**: Game developers need to handle large amounts of data efficiently, and C++

allows for manual memory management to optimize performance.
- o **Game Engines**: Many of the world's most popular game engines, such as **Unreal Engine** and **Unity** (through C#), are built with C++ at their core.
- **Key Concepts to Explore in Game Development:**
  - o **Graphics Programming**: Learn how to work with **SFML**, **SDL**, or **OpenGL** to render 2D and 3D graphics.
  - o **Physics and Collision Detection**: Implement game mechanics like gravity and collisions.
  - o **Networking**: Learn how to implement multiplayer features in games.

Resources for Learning C++ Game Development:

- **Books:**
  - o *Game Programming Patterns* by Robert Nystrom
  - o *Beginning C++ Through Game Programming* by Michael Dawson
  - o *Real-Time Rendering* by Tomas Akenine-Möller and Eric Haines
- **Online Resources:**
  - o Learn C++ Game Development with SFML
  - o C++ Game Development on Udemy

Further Reading and Resources

To keep improving your C++ skills, the following resources will help you stay up-to-date and deepen your understanding:

Books:

1. **Effective Modern C++** by Scott Meyers

- This book provides a deep dive into the new features of C++11 and C++14 and their impact on writing more efficient and maintainable code.
2. **C++ Primer** by Stanley B. Lippman
   - A great starting point for beginners, this book covers everything from basic syntax to advanced topics like templates and the Standard Library.
3. **The C++ Programming Language** by Bjarne Stroustrup
   - Written by the creator of C++, this book is an authoritative resource on the language, covering all aspects of C++ in-depth.

Online Courses:

1. **Coursera**: *C++ for C Programmers* - A fantastic course that bridges the gap between C and C++ programming.
2. **Udemy**: *Advanced C++ Programming* - This course covers advanced C++ topics, including templates, concurrency, and design patterns.

C++ Communities and Forums:

1. **Stack Overflow**: A great place to get help with C++ problems from a large and active community.
2. **Reddit's C++ Community**: Join r/cpp for discussions, news, and tips about C++.
3. **CppCon**: Attend conferences or watch videos from C++ conferences to stay updated on the latest features and best practices in C++ programming.

Words of Encouragement: Stay Persistent and Keep Building!

Learning C++ is no small feat, and the journey is only just beginning. It can sometimes feel overwhelming as you tackle advanced topics, but remember that persistence is key. Every time you encounter a challenge, think of it as an opportunity to learn something new. Stay curious, keep experimenting, and don't be afraid to make mistakes. Mistakes are simply stepping stones toward becoming a better programmer.

C++ is a powerful tool, and the more you work with it, the more confident you will become in your ability to build high-performance, scalable systems. Whether you're designing software for industries like finance, healthcare, or game development, the knowledge you've gained in this book provides a solid foundation for any project.

So, what's next? Keep exploring new libraries, frameworks, and tools that can help you build amazing applications. Don't be afraid to tackle big projects—just take them one step at a time. And most importantly, never stop learning. The C++ community is vast, and there's always more to discover.

Congratulations! You've completed the journey through this book, and now you're ready to continue your adventure with C++—a journey that will last as long as you're curious and determined. Keep building, keep learning, and enjoy the process of creating something amazing with C++!

www.ingramcontent.com/pod-product-compliance
Lightning Source LLC
LaVergne TN
LVHW022345060326
832902LV00022B/4250